HOMELESS YOUNG PEOPLE IN SCOTLAND

The Role of the Social Work Services

A Report by

The University of Glasgow

to the

Scottish Office

January 1993

Any views expressed in this report are not necessarily those of Ministers or the Department.

ISBN O 11 494227 7

The Authors

Jon Bannister
Muriel Dell
David Donnison
Suzanne Fitzpatrick
Rex Taylor

Report Contents

Introduction

Part I. The Problem

Page

Part II. Responses

Part III. Conclusions

Appendices

INTRODUCTION

This study was commissioned by the Scottish Office through its Social Work Services Group. Its purpose was to examine the role of the social work authorities in relation to the prevention and management of homelessness among young people in Scotland, with special reference to: (1) preventive action, (2) assistance at the time of initial inquiry, (3) emergency liaison with other services, and (4) the provision of accommodation and support services.

"Young people" were defined for the purposes of the study as being under the age of thirty, unmarried and without dependants. It was found that most of those who become homeless are teenagers or in their early twenties.

"Homelessness" was defined as circumstances in which people have no tolerable, safe and secure place in which to live. It includes, at one end of the spectrum, people given temporary lodging by their friends, and, at the other, people sleeping in doorways and public toilets.

The study was made by the Centre for Housing Research and the Department of Social Policy and Social Work of Glasgow University under the joint supervision of David Donnison and Rex Taylor. The principal researcher was Jon Bannister. Chapter Three of this Report, dealing with the law, was prepared by Suzanne Fitzpatrick whose work was funded by Scottish Homes. Muriel Dell made an important contribution throughout the study. Jane Morton helped us to make a special study of London and young Scots who go there. Valuable help was also given by Kay Carmichael. While this research was going on the team were invited by the Tayside Regional Council to make a similar study of the Perth and Kinross District. That was done by Gordon McAdam and presented as a separate Report, with help from members of the team. We have drawn on his work in this Report. Sheena Butler did most of our typing, besides a great deal of the administrative work required to keep the study going.

The authors gained advice from many sources, too numerous to list, most important among whom were young people who were, or had recently been, homeless. They were consulted at the beginning of the study and again when its conclusions were being prepared. Others whose help has been particularly valuable are Malcolm Hill, Richard Kinsey, Tom Mullen, Laurie Naumann and Ann Rosengard.

A Steering Committee was established to advise the researchers and the Scottish Office. Its members were: David Wishart (Chair), Sheenagh Adams, John Bishop, Amanda Britain, Anne Connor, Martyn Evans, Peter Marsden, Bill Moore and Bob Winter. They gave helpfully critical advice at all stages of the work.

The authors are grateful to all who have helped them but wish to make it clear that they alone are responsible for this Report.

This is how it is organised. Part I outlines the problems to be addressed, explaining their origins and drawing on the evidence of homeless young people to convey the realities of their situation.

Part II presents the main findings of the research in four Chapters dealing with: the law as it relates to homeless young people; the response of a sample of agencies to a set of imaginary but typical examples of potentially homeless youngsters; the work actually done on 80 such cases by these agencies; and a survey of the experience and views of staff in various agencies dealing with homeless young people.

Part III presents our conclusions and recommendations. The evidence of our research, reviewed in Chapter 7, and the experience of the experts whom we surveyed compel us to say a good deal about the housing and Social Security services which go far to shape the opportunities of homeless youngsters and hence the problems which the social work authorities deal with and the scope they have. Before presenting our recommendations about these services we outline the strategic requirements for successful work in this field and the parts which housing and Social Security services should play, along with the social work authorities, in developing that broader strategy. We bring together the discussion of these two scales of action - the strategic and the operational - in the final pages of the Chapter which deal with the law and its interpretation. Then, in Chapter 8, we present our recommendations for the social work authorities, concluding with a note on the costs and benefits of our proposals.

Part I. The Problem

Chapter 1

Setting Up Home

Introduction

Anyone seeking to understand disease must first study health, just as anyone who wants to understand crime must first learn why most people grow up to be, most of the time, law-abiding. If we do not understand the biological and social processes which shape ordinary patterns of behaviour, we cannot understand the deviant or "problem" cases.

So we start this Report by asking how it comes about that most people move out of the homes in which they were nurtured to form households of their own. The Chapter is divided into three parts. After distinguishing the main motives and influences at work, and showing the importance of the links between them, we examine, in a second section, the ways in which the process operates for different kinds of people. That analysis begins to suggest why some people are more likely than others to become homeless, at least for a while, when they try to set up households of their own. Finally, in a third section, we ask why homelessness has become more common among young people than it used to be only a few years ago. If the argument and evidence we have presented are sound, they should throw some light on this question.

Setting up home

Young people fortunate enough to be cared for by good parents in a comfortable home have strong reasons for staying where they are. The marginal costs of sheltering someone in a home that is already fully equipped are much less than those of setting up a new one. Even if the costs of independent living can be met, it takes a great deal of time and energy to learn to cook, repair the house, tend the garden, deal with landlords and neighbours, pay the bills and acquire all the other skills which the experienced householder takes for granted. Meanwhile parents may feel that their children offer them emotional and financial support which they are reluctant to lose. Since these anchoring factors are plainly powerful, the first question to ask is not How, but *Why* does anyone leave home?

Three sets of factors will be in play. Pull factors encourage youngsters to leave. The search for a sexual partner may drive them out of neighbourhoods where there is no compatible person of their age available. When they find a partner both of them will want space and privacy. Young people will also seek training and jobs which may not be available within reach of their parents' homes. The search for adventure, for friends and for opportunities of exploring the world – these too draw them away from home.

Push factors may be important too. Parents may want more space, privacy and an end to child-rearing responsibilities – particularly if they have increasingly heavy responsibilities for frail older relatives whom they may have to bring into their homes, or if they have broken up and the parent left in the home has a new partner. Step relationships are often stressful for all concerned; both generations may find it easier to cope if they do not have to live within the same house.

When young people leave home they need support of various kinds to help them find their feet successfully. It is normal at this stage to find them returning to their parents' homes for periods of a few weeks or months, or just for the weekend. One researcher has made a useful distinction between those who are "living away from home", while retaining the option of returning at any time, and those who have "left home", and only return as visitors.[1] But the transition from one status to the other is often gradual, and the distinction between them may not be clearly defined even by the people concerned. Sometimes other relatives, or friends from an older generation – surrogate parents – provide the support needed at this stage. Besides this help – as much emotional as practical – young people need shelter which they can afford; the comradeship of friends; and a modest but sufficient income from earnings, student grants, social security payments or other reliable sources.

When the combination of pull, push and supporting factors grows strong enough to outweigh the ties which anchor them at home, young people move out. But the transition is rarely swift and complete. There may be a long period when they think of their parents' house as "home", rely on the support it affords them and return often to it, before they establish a lasting and secure home of their own. Evelyn Waugh, in his first novel, vividly describes this period and the reluctance of Captain Grimes, his anti-hero, to move on to the next phase. At the stag party held on the eve of his wedding, Grimes says "Our life is lived between two homes ... We emerge for a little into the light, and then the front door closes ... There's a home and family waiting for every one of us ... each of us unconsciously pregnant with desirable villa residences".[2]

This is not a model which provides simple, predictive equations showing when new households will form and how successfully they will achieve the transition. That is partly because the formation of a new household is a more gradual and less sharply defined process than the appearance of a new entry on the Community Charge register; partly because the transition calls for a complex combination of the factors we have rather crudely categorised; and partly because opportunities vary greatly from place to place. One researcher has estimated from General Household Survey data of 1979 that the average gap between leaving home and becoming the head of a new household is one year.[3] But such averages, as we shall see, are apt to conceal more than they reveal.

Quite different housing markets operate alongside each other in the same places. It is usually easier to find housing which is suitable for small, mobile, newly-formed households in the inner parts of big cities than in smaller places. But the housing which is publicly advertised and available to newcomers is usually much more expensive than that secured by long-established residents who know the ropes.[4] In London, where rents and house prices are particularly high and good jobs for newcomers are scarce, it is difficult to get a secure and decent home unless you have helpful personal contacts, or have accumulated many points on a council waiting list, or form a household with two earners and few dependants, or hold a reasonably well-paid job which probably requires a good deal of training. That list of options suggests some of the different strategies which lead to the successful establishment of new households. In other cities where housing is more plentiful in relation to demand, the transition is easier. In small towns and villages it is rare for young people to be homeless,[5] but that does not mean that local citizens do not become homeless. It may only mean that those who have difficulties in finding housing move on – and are encouraged by local officials to move on – to larger cities where they believe they will have a better chance of getting shelter.

Contrasting patterns

The routes which young people follow as they move towards independence vary from place to place, and according to gender and class.

Young women tend to leave home sooner than young men. In the cohort, born in 1958, which is being monitored by the National Child Development Study, 65% of men and 84% of women had left their parental homes by the age of 23 (defining that home as wherever they were living at the age of sixteen). The median age at leaving was 21.9 for men and 20 for women.[6] The main reason for this difference is the predominance of marriage amongst the reasons for leaving home, coupled with the fact that wives are, on average, about two years younger than their husbands.

Looking only at those leaving home for the first time, the first to go – before the age of 18 – most frequently gave the search for a job as their main reason. That pattern was particularly common among men. The reason most often given by the next leavers – aged 18-19 – was to become a student; again a reason given most often by men. Older leavers gave the decision to live as a married person as their main reason for leaving home. "Negative" reasons, such as friction or overcrowding at home, were most frequently given by the youngest leavers – 25% of those departing before they were eighteen, and thereafter by declining numbers.

Men and women with middle class parents leave home sooner, on average, than those with working class parents, but that difference is entirely accounted for by the larger numbers in the middle class who leave to become students. Most of these will be "living away from home" rather than "leaving home". Since they return home quite frequently, they are, in effect, getting a gentle training in the art of setting up on their own.

People in professional and managerial jobs tend to operate in a national – sometimes an international – economy, while manual workers tend to operate in an urban or regional economy, seeking work and housing within daily travelling distance of their original homes.[7] That difference starts early in life, with the search for training opportunities which often compels middle class youngsters to leave home. Universities, colleges and some of the major employers of young trainees give youngsters some help in finding housing. Thus students benefit from supports which are less likely to be available to people leaving home for other reasons. Because their families are more likely to have moved around the country in earlier years, middle class youngsters are also more likely than their working class contemporaries to find supportive relatives living nearby if they move to distant places.

This evidence deals only with the first move away from home. Half those who say they first left for work or for training return home for at least six months, and nearly half (45%) of those who left for negative reasons do likewise. It is those who leave to get married who are most likely to have really "left home". Working class people moving away from their parents are more likely than the middle class to live with other relatives, and more likely to find a home close to their parents. The middle class are more likely to live with unrelated people, as many of them learnt to do in their student days.

"The pattern which is now emerging", says the author of the most comprehensive recent report on these things, "is of working class young people leaving the parental home usually on a permanent basis, for marriage (in which case they move into the marital home). Among the middle class the picture is different, with temporary moves away from the parental home which are not associated with marriage and which result in most young people sharing with their peers some form of intermediate, independent housing, unless the initial move from the parental home is for the purpose of marriage. When the stable working class [meaning those in which both the parents and their young depend on working class jobs] leave home for reasons other than marriage, they follow a pattern which is similar to that of the stable middle class, but are more likely to live with kin."[8]

Middle class youngsters tend to move from their parents' homes into transitional housing of various kinds: furnished and unfurnished privately rented housing, shared tenancies, hostels and student housing. That transitional stage is particularly common among men, and it may last for a long time. Leaving home, forming a conventional household, getting married and starting a family may be spread over a decade. Owner-occupied housing is their eventual destination, but that often compels them to postpone and restrict child-bearing.

Working class youngsters more rarely get into transitional housing. They move more often from their parents' homes into family housing – leaving home, getting married and starting a family being crammed into a short period of a year or so. About half of them buy a home, and about a third get into social rented housing. Although there is some movement between these tenures, they stand more often as the terminal points of people's housing careers. While house buyers postpone child-bearing, council tenants start their families sooner and have more children – the causal links between tenure and fertility operating in both directions.

There appears to be a growing demand for transitional housing, which may be as urgently sought by working class as by middle class youngsters, but more rarely found by them.

Homelessness

Most housing is second-hand. Someone else lived in it before the present occupants, and a new generation is already queuing up to succeed to it. If people become homeless, that is because they have been excluded in the game of musical chairs which leads successive cohorts through this market. The evidence we have presented suggests where the danger points lie which may entrap the losers in this game.

Setting up a new household is an expensive and complex task which has to be learnt, like any other. Those who have to move straight into independent living early, without much preparation and with little support from family or friends, or from institutions which have an interest in their health and happiness, are more likely than most to get into difficulties. Those who are pushed out of home early by conflicts and overcrowding will be particularly vulnerable. It is normal for young people to return – often many times – to their parents' homes before setting up a secure home of their own. Those who have no refuge of this kind to shelter them if things go wrong are likely to become homeless.

Ideally, education and training precede regular, paid work; reasonably paid work precedes long-term commitment to a partner; and a period of steady work by two earners, unburdened by dependants, who together secure and equip a home precedes child-bearing. We do not offer these as moral prescriptions: we simply note that the housing market operates – and is related to the markets for education and employment – in ways which make life easier for young people who are able to take things in this order. Those who have children before they secure a lasting life partner or a decent job, and those who have to leave home and seek work before they can secure a good training compete in this market at a grave disadvantage.

All these pitfalls will be harder to avoid in places where house prices are very high; where rented housing, available on demand, is very scarce; where unemployment and low-paid work are common; and where there are a lot of vulnerable newcomers who lack the support of nearby relatives and a good knowledge of the local housing market. London is an extreme example of these conditions.

Contending with these handicaps in difficult places, people are liable to become homeless. But what does that mean? We regard it as the condition of those who have no decent, adequate shelter in which they are entitled to remain and can safely live. That is what the legislation on the subject effectively means. The most extreme cases are *roofless*, sleeping rough in parks, railway stations and doorways. Others are in housing which is *insecure*, or physically *intolerable*, or – for social reasons – *unsafe* for them.

Homelessness is hard to define in a generally accepted fashion. Data about the homeless are not broken down in ways which provide reliable evidence about numbers or trends for particular groups. Nevertheless, all the experts in this field agree that the numbers of young, childless people who become homeless – many of them teenagers – have increased rapidly over the past decade.

Scottish Office figures show a rise of 124% in the numbers of homeless households seeking help and an increase of 101% in the numbers actually assessed as homeless between 1979/80 and 1990/91. These figures, being based on applications to local housing authorities, represent a flow of households becoming homeless during the year. They may be affected by changing recording practices. Shelter (Scotland) provides different estimates – generally about 15% higher – but the two coincided during the year 1990/91 at about 34,600. Of these, 44%, or 14,900 were single people, according to official figures; and of these 7,780 were under 25, with 2,960 under 18. There are likely to be many more who are effectively homeless but not recorded as such because they do not apply for help. We know that some of these are in the extreme roofless category.[9]

Why has this increase come about? Using the model outlined at the start of this Chapter, it is possible to identify some of the trends which explain this change. Look first at the pull factors. The labour market has, since the mid-'seventies, become increasingly divided with, on the one hand, a well-paid, secure core of well-trained workers and, on the other, a growing margin of people in insecure, low-paid jobs or unemployed. The long-term tendency of capitalism gradually to bring about a more equal distribution of income and wealth[10] has, since the early 1970s, been reversed. That reversal, to be seen in most of the countries of the O.E.C.D., has in Britain been exacerbated by policies for incomes and the corporate management of the economy, and by changes in taxes and benefits which have together given this country a bigger increase in poverty and inequality than any other country of the E.C.[11] There are a lot more poor people about than there were a few years ago – and the biggest increase has taken place among families with dependent children.

Between 1979 and 1989 the number of Scottish people depending on income support increased by 77% to 799,000. Of these, about one-third were aged under 16. This represents 22% of the child population of Scotland.[12] Another official source estimates that 28% of children under 16 in Scotland were dependent on income support in 1990. If allowance is made for the families entitled to income support who were not claiming it, that figure would be 34%.[13] Clearly Scottish families and their children have come under growing economic pressures.

Meanwhile, in the housing market, there has been a steady growth in one-person households – a growth now more than three times as fast as the growth in total households. The younger among them used to rely mainly on privately rented accommodation, available on demand to people who do not have to demonstrate officially recognised needs. But this has continued to dwindle.[14] New tenancies are now largely freed from rent controls so their rents have risen sharply. New private housing for rent, built with the help of the Business Expansion Scheme, is let at high rents, far out of reach of the homeless. Meanwhile, the virtual cessation of council building, and the sale to sitting tenants of large numbers of council houses – particularly concentrated in the places where public housing was already most scarce – have weakened the capacity of many local authorities to fulfil their duties to the homeless.

Some local authorities have tried, despite these difficulties, to offer housing to homeless young people. But the houses most readily available are rarely in the most accessible and supportive neighbourhoods. And a house, by itself, is not a home. To make a home, youngsters venturing into the world for the first time need the kind of support that more fortunate young people can expect to receive from their families. Who will provide this for the less fortunate? Local housing authorities – compelled on the one hand to house a growing proportion of the more vulnerable tenants and, on the other, to adopt increasingly hard-nosed, commercial patterns of management – have been uncertain how to respond to those needs.

Meanwhile in the owner-occupied market, the rise in land prices and interest rates and the drastic reduction in house-building which have taken place in the last few years have held up the forward movement of the queue of households waiting to buy a home. The poorer of the young people following behind them in the next cohort, waiting to rent transitional housing, are thus more likely to fall out of the game into homelessness.

Some of the more important supports which help young people to get started have been removed in recent years. The widespread reductions in social security benefits – both in regular weekly allowances, and in payments for exceptional needs such as furniture and household equipment, and in the treatment of rent and community charge payments – have been particularly focused on young people seeking to set up home for the first time. Meanwhile the community charge loads a new burden on the same young people when they are over eighteen. These changes in benefits and in taxation have encouraged more young people to keep on the move, making it harder than ever for them to negotiate their way into the public or private sectors of the housing market.

For some young people, the push factors – what researchers have called the "negative reasons" for leaving home – have been sharpened. More and more of them are growing up in families in which the parents have split up and the one remaining with the youngster has taken a new partner. Research based on data from the National Child Development Study, which is tracing the progress of a large cohort of children born in 1958, shows that these step relationships are much more likely to lead to trouble of various kinds for the young people concerned – early departure from home for negative reasons, early departure from school without qualifications, unemployment, and so on.[15] Meanwhile cuts in the social security benefits which these youngsters used to bring into the home have made them a less attractive financial asset for the household to which they belong. It is hard to say whether physical and sexual abuse have become more common within families than they used to be, or only more frankly discussed. They figure frequently in the experience of the homeless youngsters whom we met.

These trends help to explain why there was a big increase in the numbers of children and young people entering public care during the years between 1985 and 1988.[16] Although those numbers have been falling again more recently, the young people who came into care earlier are now emerging – many of them bursting to escape, but lacking the support provided by a normal family which allows its children to "live away from home" for many years and return repeatedly to the nest before finally taking wing to "leave home".

It is not possible to quantify the influence of these developments at all precisely, but together they must increase the strength of the "push factors" ejecting many of the more vulnerable young people into a harsh world, and weaken the constructive "pull factors" and the essential "supports" available to help them set up a home for themselves. It would be very surprising if homelessness among the young had not increased during recent years. Since these trends were not foreseen when our present public services took shape, it would also be very surprising if these services were well organised to help homeless young people.

Notes

1 D. Leonard, *Sex and Generation: a Study of Courtship and Weddings*, Tavistock, London, 1980.

2 Evelyn Waugh, *Decline and Fall*, Penguin Books, 1960, p.102.

3 M. Anderson, *Family Structure in Nineteenth Century Lancashire*, Cambridge University Press, 1971.

4 *Report of the Committee on Housing in Greater London*, Cmnd.2605, HMSO, 1965, p.291.

5 Scottish Homes have recently commissioned studies of housing in rural areas which support this conclusion.

6 Gill Jones, "Leaving the Parental Home: An Analysis of Early Housing Careers", *Journal of Social Policy*, 16, 1; pp.49-74.

7 Department of the Environment, *Housing Policy*, Technical Volume, Part I, pp.95 and 98, 1976.

8 Gill Jones, op. cit., pp.65-66.

9 For data on homelessness in Scotland, see Scottish Office Central Research Unit Paper, *Homelessness in Scotland*, September 1990; Scottish Homes Information Paper, *Homelessness in Scotland*, 1991; Shelter (Scotland), *Scottish Housing Monitor*, March/April 1992; and Scottish Council for Single Homeless, *Manifesto for Single Homeless People*, March 1992.

10 Henry Phelps Brown, *The Inequality of Pay*, Oxford University Press, 1977.

11 "Eurostat" data. See also Ruut Veenhoven et al. (editors), *Did the Crisis Really Hurt?* D. Reidel, Dordrecht, 1991.

12 Data from the Benefits Agency, quoted in recent unpublished study by Save the Children Fund (Scotland).

13 Data from Lothian Regional Council Health Committee (1990) quoted by Save the Children Fund (Scotland). See also Strathclyde Poverty Alliance, Youth Destitution in Strathclyde, 1992.

14 *Social Trends*, H.M.S.O.

15 We are indebted to Kath Kiernan at the Family Policy Studies Centre, London, for evidence on this point. Some of her work is briefly summarised in "What About the Children?" *Family Policy Bulletin*, December, 1991.

16 *Social Trends*, H.M.S.O.

Chapter 2

Young People Speak For Themselves

Introduction

Before beginning our research on the work of public services concerned with homeless young people we had to gain an understanding of their situation from the young people themselves. In a series of in-depth discussions the pathways of a group of young homeless Scots have been monitored. The interviews helped to sensitize the researchers to the nature of homelessness, and whilst they form only a small non-random sample, very clear and consistent strands of experience were identified. The findings illuminate points at which social work departments (and other similarly charged agencies) might usefully intervene to prevent or ameliorate the impact of homelessness. It is evident, from these commentaries, that young people who experience homelessness are powerless, afraid, and dependent upon the help of others. Recognising this makes it essential to provide the opportunity for young people to speak for themselves.

In total, 35 people, ranging in age from 16 to 30, participated in this component of the research programme. They were interviewed in eight small groups, one of which was located in London. They were contacted through agencies working in the field of homelessness in both Strathclyde and Lothian regions, and in London. The majority had become roofless directly upon leaving the parental home, the remainder had a care or institution background.

At the outset, it must be stressed that the young people who participated in the discussions must not be assumed to be the most vulnerable of the young homeless groups. First, they had received some form of assistance, and were on the whole in supported accommodation. Second, these were people who had the self-confidence to come forward and articulate their views. Their accounts of family life and of their reluctance to leave home until they were compelled by intolerable circumstances to do so suggested to us that their less able or courageous siblings were left behind – and may suffer as a result.

The following table (Pathways to Independence: Interview format) highlights the key issues discussed and the focus upon which each section was aimed. The format of the interview schedule has been adopted as the structure of this Chapter. Further sections are devoted to the experience of homeless Scots in London, and the advice that the young homeless would offer to peers and the helping agencies.

Table 2.1:   Pathways to Independence: Interview format

Issues for discussion	Focus
Motivation(s) for leaving home Planning move from home (or care) Attempts to prevent the onset of homelessness	Origin
Becoming homeless (the timing) Difficulties upon leaving home and the experience of rooflessness	Experience
Coping (short term)	Management
Managing Independent living and the future	Aspirations and Expectations

Notes:

1 This format has been designed to trace pathways into and out of homelessness.
2 At this stage only a crude distinction will be drawn between the related concepts of rooflessness and homelessness (the "spectrum" of homelessness was discussed in Chapter 1). Rooflessness may be defined as being without access to any form of accommodation. Homelessness is defined to include also the situation of those whose shelter is physically intolerable, insecure or unsafe.

Motivations for leaving home

The first topic of discussion concentrated on the reasons young people gave for leaving home. It was evident that the majority of those interviewed felt that they had been driven from home by intolerable circumstances. The conversations revolved around two major themes, continual family arguments, and the presence or intermittent threat of physical or sexual abuse.

The first theme was that of family disputes. Usually several arguments culminated in one major dispute which led to the young person leaving or being thrown out. Disagreements often focused upon a poor relationship with a natural parent's current partner (i.e. stepfather/mother). It must be remembered that most of these young people – and often their parents and step-parents too – were unemployed. Overcrowding is easier to bear if most of the household are out at work all day during the week, and earn money with which to go out at weekends too. It would be unfair to suggest that the blame for disputes was placed entirely upon the parents; there was an acute awareness amongst those interviewed of the financial and overcrowding stress in the family home. Eventually, however, one major dispute led to the breakdown of the family unit. As Clare (18) explained,

> *"It's the pressure, it's constant, you try to please them (parents) and whatever you're doing, you're doing wrong"*

Obviously, family disputes occurring through adolescence are a common feature of all families. However, the combination of difficulties, including arguments with step-parents, parental drink problems, financial pressure, lack of wider family support, all of which were expressed by group participants, either made them resolve to leave home or, as was also the case, they were thrown out. Most had heard the phrase,

"and if you don't like it, you know where the door is!"

Those who experienced abuse felt that the *only* solution lay in them taking the initiative and escaping from home. They complained that no one outside the home appeared to interpret their "bruises" and "broken limbs" to be the result of beatings. Some stated that they left so that their younger brothers and sisters did not have to witness such beatings and come to believe this to be a "normal" process of growing up. Others left afraid that if their plight was brought to the attention of the authorities, not only would they be placed in greater physical danger, but the younger children would be taken away into care. As James (18) commented,

"I left to avoid the doings"

Planning the move from home/care

> **"When I left, I left in a bit of a rush. I didn't have time to plan anything. I did have it in the back of my head to leave, but the situation at that time was such that I just had to go. Because everything happened so fast I didn't even have any time to pack anything. I just grabbed a jacket and a couple of shirts, put them in a bag, and I was off."** (Stuart 19)

Although many knew that ultimately they would have to leave, no one could predict when the final big argument would precipitate the need to get out as fast as possible. This, combined with a lack of resources, both financial and social (family and friends), usually meant that the final break was unprepared.

The key factor here is that the problems at home were regarded as far more difficult or dangerous than any of the difficulties they might experience in the "unknown" upon leaving. Except for those who were leaving a care institution, only one person was able to make contact with an agency prior to leaving. The majority felt unable to discuss or plan the move with either family friends or any formal agency prior to leaving, as events unfolded so quickly. The various experiences may best be summarised as follows by Sharon (17).

> **"I knew for a long time that I was leaving, but what I was going to do when I left was another matter. As soon as I was out the door I didn't have a clue where I was going. All I knew was that I had a chance to leave all that (the beatings) behind me."**

Leaving care, just like leaving the parental home, can be a traumatic experience. Having to manage independently at the age of 16 is extremely difficult. To this end, some element of planning prior to leaving care and follow-up support is crucial to ensuring a successful move into the community. This process, however, often takes place in a strained atmosphere with the young person anxious to leave care behind them. Whilst some of those interviewed were fortunate and gained access to a "halfway-house", and maintained contact with previous carers (including Social Workers), the remainder expressed a degree of bitterness that after-care support was, for them, non-existent.

Those who left care and went directly into their own tenancy had no idea what to expect. These tenancies rapidly broke down, a result of limited experience of the practical aspects of day-to-day living. Having limited independence whilst in care, and spending their days with a considerable number of other young people, they were suddenly expected to be adults and manage on their own and alone. These people said that they were "doomed" before they started.

Attempts to prevent the onset of homelessness

Several made attempts to return home. They were lonely, missed their families, and destitute. Those who did return, and an observable pattern of return existed, found that conditions had not improved; the "rules" had been made harder. The new arrangements invariably broke down and once more they had to leave. The message is clear. Deborah (17) said that,

> *"You can't go back because you don't want to. Some do go back but it never works out."*

Staying with friends or relatives from the extended family group was also attempted, yet the financial and overcrowding pressures which existed in the family home often persisted here, and, after a while most had to leave.

Becoming homeless

All were asked at what stage they had considered themselves as being homeless. It was thought that the acceptance of being homeless would take time to "sink in", recognition being delayed until contact was made with a helping agency. This was not found to be the case; they knew immediately that they were homeless because of the very real survival questions that they faced. Karen (21) explained,

> *"As soon as you're out the door you know that you're homeless. You're frightened and you don't know how you're going to survive."*

Difficulties upon leaving and the experience of rooflessness

The discussion then turned to consider the experience of rooflessness. This stage was entered in a state of confusion, the young people not knowing what to expect. The only certainty they faced was that they could not go back. Simon (18) explained,

> *"I was wandering about, wondering what on earth happened. I was just in this daze thinking I've walked out and I can't go back. What on earth do I do now?"*

Some spent the first night away from home sleeping rough. Of those that slept rough, this lasted for between two nights and three months. The immediate need was to find somewhere sheltered from the elements (a doorway, a close, a toilet), which was also "safe". They did not sleep properly during this period, as they were afraid what might happen to them if they did.

All were extremely lonely, feeling that they had no one to talk to. They were outcasts and felt shunned by members of the public. Gary (18) explained,

"People will walk by you. They could be heading right for you then they will look up and see you and change direction. Because they must think you are going to ask them for something. I wasn't going to ask them for anything."

One of the most pressing problems was a lack of money. This was due, in part, to the unplanned departure from the parental home. This observation has to be married to the fact that young people, especially those under 18 years of age, have very limited access to benefits and other resources.

Access to benefits was a continual matter for concern. Most commented on the long delays before they received payments, and that when they eventually did receive some money it was not sufficient to make ends meet. They told stories of having to walk all over town, fruitlessly trying to get their benefits sorted out. Finding work was impossible with no fixed abode. Attempting to get money through the severe hardship allowance was variously described as a "very painful experience", and like trying to "get blood out of a stone". Several stated that they were,

"afraid to go to the interview and get interrogated."

A consequence of a lack of money is the inability to purchase food. Most young roofless and homeless people have very limited diets, suffer considerable weight loss, and face diet related health problems. Steven (17), explained that when he slept rough he,

"made three pounds and eighty pence last ten days. I only ate Twixs and Mars Bars. They're cheap. They don't fill you up, but they keep you going."

When they were hungry and had no money to buy food, the options available were very unpleasant. Some said that they resorted to begging. They claimed that many of the young people on the streets have to go through this degrading experience. They were,

"Just doing it through desperation" (Gary, 18)

A further alternative mentioned was petty crime. These stories were told with bravado, yet nevertheless represented a grim reality. You could,

"take to crime, or put a brick through a window. You get a record but at least you'll have something in your stomach" (Sarah, 21),

or similarly you could resort to stealing, taking,

"whatever you could fit in your pocket, like frozen sausages and hamburgers" (Sharon, 17)

Other important aspects of life became marginalised during this period of time. Health care, for example, was regarded as,

"the least of your worries when you're out on the street" (Deborah, 17)

Most thought that they could get to see a doctor in an emergency, although they doubted whether this access extended to other services, such as dentistry. Whilst all interviewees attempted to maintain cleanliness, this often proved difficult, and was treated as a secondary concern to eating and finding somewhere to sleep.

Self-confidence and pride were eroded in this period. They felt awkward. Even if they did not "care what others thought" about them, they considered themselves to be outcasts, and were uncomfortable going into public places. The only people they had something in common with were other roofless people, and where possible (if such contacts were made) they would team up for mutual support.

Coping

The discussions then turned to evaluate the approaches made to, and the responses of, various helping agencies. Of particular interest to us was the role of the social work departments. Ideally, this stage would represent the first step towards stability, and the basic needs of the young people would be met. It is important to note that, initially, the various helping agencies were avoided, or not known. Youngsters were both frightened and suspicious of the potential outcomes of making contact, and they did not want to appear to be begging. It must be remembered that these youngsters had already had very bad experience with adults. That is why they left home. David (19) said that,

> *"I didn't want to tell anyone I had left home, I was too embarrassed. I didn't want someone to batter out questions to me that I didn't want to answer."*

or similarly,

> *"I was too frightened to go, I was frightened about what they would ask. I didn't want to answer any questions"* (Gary, 18)

Eventually contact was made upon the advice received from other homeless people or through chance contact with an agency. Of all the statutory agencies, the social work department, along with the police, were the last with which they made contact. Most only thought of approaching the housing department. The social work department was distrusted and disliked. Franceen (17) stated that when she left home she,

> *"Didn't go to the Social Work Department because of the reputation they have. I had it in my mind that if I went to the Social Work Department, I would either be dragged back home again, or I would be flung in a children's home, even though I was sixteen. I still had it in my mind that they would fling me in an institution."*

Others described their perception based upon family information,

> *"My family didn't believe in Social Work. They said that if you get a social worker to help you then they (social workers) would always be hunting you down for help back"* (Paul, 17)

Social workers were viewed as directive and exploitative, and many young people were frightened that social workers would try to re-integrate them with their family without their permission.

Some were initially "assigned" social workers as a result of their previous care background, age, or defined vulnerability. In the beginning, social workers were perceived as not to be trusted and were at best unhelpful. There were complaints of a lack of confidentiality and a lack of availability. Some felt that social workers would provide support "sometimes", others felt that social workers were lazy, they did not know what it was like to be roofless or homeless, and they could do much more if they tried harder.

Social workers were seen as necessary only in so far as they could help secure access to benefits, and play a part in securing more permanent supported accommodation. They felt that if a social worker was with them then it became far easier to get money. They were bitter that this was the case, and described it as blatantly unfair. Without the authority of a social worker, everyone would, "Treat you like a big wean" (Clare, 18) and tell you that,

> *"you're all just a problem, you're all delinquents – not old enough to know what is happening to you."* (Mary, 16)

and that as a result,

> **"You have not got the ability to stand on your own two feet because no one gives you a chance to do so."** (Jamie, 17)

Although receiving some form of assistance, many still rely on family contacts for a modicum of financial support and advice. One young person still meets his mother, who gives him money for cigarettes, every morning. This meeting has to take place undercover, as her boyfriend would "raise hell" if he discovered she was in contact with her son. Those that were able to maintain contact with their family found that it provided invaluable support in these very difficult times, even if it was just to get "things off your chest". Friends were less of a help, particularly because they had no idea of the problems faced by roofless people. Their concerns were those of teenagers. Peter (20) stated that,

> **"I had explained to friends what was happening, but they were too interested in their own lives to help me. Most of my friends were people that I just went about with. I couldn't go to any of them for help, they would close the front door on you."**

Managing

The transition from a short stay hostel to more secure supported accommodation is not straightforward. It is dependent upon a vacancy being available and a successful referral being made. The young people interviewed cited several instances when a projected move had broken down. Yet these were the successful applicants; they all had progressed to more stable accommodation.

Places were found in a variety of hostels and tenancies, varying in the type of support offered and the duration of stay permitted. Those that applied for tenancies were reasonably happy about the initial response of housing authorities to their plight, but fewer were pleased with the subsequent offers made. First, they had to wait a long time for an offer. Second, when one was made it tended to be in the remote areas of the city. Once again these tenancies ran the risk of breaking down in the short term.

Mixed views existed as to the quality of the hostel places offered, and a distinction needs to be drawn between the short and the long term hostel placing. The same short term hostels were variously described as "dangerous" because of the drug abuse and violence thought to be present, or "good" because they provided 24 hour staff. No strong conclusions can be taken from the experience of the short term hostels, except that there was general concern expressed that young people were often inappropriately placed with older more "dangerous" residents.

The longer term hostels enabled people to begin both planning and preparing for the future. As Christine (23) expressed, at last,

> **"You can start living your life the way it should be, the way it should have been from the very start. Just carry on and get yourself a job."**

In addition to counselling (where appropriate) a range of practical help and advice was provided in these hostels. This included information on diet, cooking, budgeting and making applications for permanent accommodation. Once again there was a mixed interpretation as to how helpful these services were: some reported regular contact with "key" workers whilst others felt they had to get on and "do their own thing".

Even with good preparation, some percentage of breakdown is inevitable and support arrangements must allow for this and be flexible to the diverse demands of young people. The timing of a move into a permanent tenancy was also a matter of concern. Whilst some felt that they were being held back, others were afraid that they would be pushed out before they were ready and would lose the support that they were presently receiving. They were worried that the subsequent "pressure" and "isolation" would be difficult to cope with. It must be remembered that most young people who never experience homelessness rely on the support of parents to whom they often return for short or long periods before finally leaving home.

Independent living and the future

> **"I just want to be able to put all this behind me, put it down to experience, and close the book."** (Jamie, 17)

The interviews then progressed to encourage participants to explore both their aspirations and their expectations for the future, and in particular, the independent living environment to which they would strive. Participants were asked to describe their ideal home. David (20), said that an ideal home would be,

> **"a place of your own with your own things around you, which provides you with comfort and security."**

Not surprisingly, when the turbulent and dangerous backgrounds of these young people are considered, the desire for a safe social and physical environment was considered to be of utmost importance.

The notion of "security" contained two related facets. First, that of security of tenure,

"You need your own house so nobody can fling you out!" (Pauline, 20)

The second element was that of physical security from criminal risk. Repeatedly, the characteristics of a prospective neighbourhood and its residents were mentioned. The location of any home would,

"need to be in a nice area, with nice people" (Steven, 17)

or similarly,

"in a half-decent area, which was cosy, liveable and safe" (David, 20)

or once again,

"a small house on a quiet street, with no bother off anyone".

To hold aspirations such as these is not unique. These are everyone's goals. Very few of these youngsters, however, believed this objective to be attainable or realistic in the short term. The need for a transitional period with support, a result of limited personal finances or social support networks, was recognised.

Despite such normal desires, the level of expectations attached to the chances of attaining these goals in the long term varied considerably. Some held very low expectations as to the security of their future accommodation, and the likelihood of having a "decent" job. This realistic assessment, however unpleasant it may be, recognises that, for many, the social and economic vulnerability which precipitated the onset of homelessness will remain even when an independent living environment has been entered. Other goals for the future matched those held by most people: some wanted to go to college, and some to have children and "settle down".

As well as expressing their hopes, these young people expressed some quite legitimate concerns for the future. First, they were concerned that because of their experiences they might be "labelled" at a later date. They were concerned, for example, that if future neighbours learned about their previous experience of being homeless they would immediately be regarded as "bad" people, and hence inherit a deviant reputation.

Second, the problem of loneliness was once again stressed. They were worried that once they moved into their own accommodation, and the support networks they were currently receiving were cut, they would become very isolated. Mark (19), who had previously held his own tenancy, but was unable to sustain it on that occasion and subsequently returned to the homeless scene, expressed these fears succinctly,

"You cannot put the loneliness into words. You sit in your flat because you cannot go anywhere, because you don't know the area and your friends live too far away".

The most frequent concern, however, related to the ever-present threat of becoming homeless or in extreme cases roofless once more. Anthony (27), when asked what his greatest fear for the future was, commented, *"being made homeless again, because there's always a chance that you will (become homeless). I'm in a minimum supported hostel at the moment and funding is always running out. I've already been in one hostel that closed down on me."*

The hopes and fears of these young people differ little from those of people their own age who have never encountered homelessness, although perhaps there is a sharper sense of reality. Their traumatic backgrounds have made them only too aware of the dangers young people face when they are forced to leave the parental home or their after care arrangements break down. They are afraid that they will become trapped on the Youth Training Scheme, "just making cups of tea", while the scheme prevents them from applying for "real" jobs and pays less than being on the dole.

Homeless Scots in London

This section will consider the experiences of young Scots who have moved to London. Eight young scottish men, aged between 18-30 (but mostly mid-20s), were interviewed at the Borderline project set up in London by the Church of Scotland. This group were representative in terms of sex and age of the majority of Borderline clients, 95% of whom are young men and very few of whom are under 18.

The whole of this group had already left home whilst in Scotland, prior to their move to London. This was a mature group with considerable work and other adult experiences behind them. Keith (26) had the impression, that,

"home was a long time ago."

The motivations behind their exodus to London focused upon the "uselessness" of Youth Training Schemes, and the lack of any proper work openings in Scotland. Most also talked about being benefit dependent, and the difficulties this imposed when attempting to move into private accommodation.

Few of those interviewed had actively planned their move to London. Only two had jobs to come to, and only one a bed (with a London based brother). The other five came down without any advance arrangements hoping to find work. In no case, however, was the move an impulse. London had been very positively chosen as a place where they had a better chance of finding work, or better work. Everything else they wanted was seen to flow from access to decently paid employment. Several had lived in London before.

All expected that finding accommodation upon arrival in London would be a problem. When asked if they had thought of seeking advice or help from within Scotland, there was general surprise. They questioned whether such advice or help existed. Despite a lack of forward planning, most seemed to have budgeted for the fare, by coach or rail. Only two mentioned having a quantity of money saved for their arrival in London. Of those who had made arrangements prior to moving south, none had contingency plans against these plans breaking down.

The most immediate and baffling problem faced was finding out who ran anything and the seemingly hostile uncaringness of Londoners. As Kenny (20) put it,

"No one wants to know if you even just ask a question in a Scots accent."

Arriving at coach and rail stations, they found no one in any kind of position of authority knowledgeable enough, or even interested, to help them. One found a list of hostels by thinking to go to a public library and consult the Directory of London Hostels. He walked, that day, from King's Cross to the Elephant and Castle and on out to Hammersmith before he found a bed for the night. Some others thought to go to the CAB. They said they were given out-of-date information and, even there, treated with some coolness. Several reported being told to,

"go home where you belong."

Members of the group had been homeless in London for periods ranging from 2 weeks to five years, with cases clustering around 6 months and three years. All had spent time sleeping rough, stayed in night shelters and in short stay hostels (3-7 days). Most had moved between shelters and hostels for extended periods. Among those in London for several years there seems to have been movement between these arrangements and a stay in medium term hostels. None of the group had entered long term secure accommodation.

The majority of this group had expected to encounter a series of difficulties upon arrival. The most unexpected problem, however, was that of finding work. This arose in two ways. First, there was the problem of holding down any work from a starting position of rooflessness. One informant claimed he had lost a job because of the lack of sleep and the problem of presenting decently. Second, it was quickly appreciated that it had to be very well-paid work to cover accommodation costs, if accommodation could be found. William (24) explained, that you could,

"<u>not</u> take something paying less than £90 a week."

Our impression is that catering is the only industry in London still offering jobs to unqualified young people, but these jobs are insecure and do not pay enough to enable anyone to get accommodation unaided. The youngsters we met all got on to the "network" of helping organisations by word of mouth among other homeless people in London, often after days or even weeks sleeping rough. Only voluntary agencies were approached. This group had never thought to approach the statutory housing or social work services in London. The key thing required was accessible, stable, temporary accommodation. This became the first goal displacing the search for employment. Apart from Borderline, most were quite cynical about the sort of "advice" that provides shelter and a bed for only one night. The underlying problem here is that there is simply not enough temporary accommodation. Several had noted that there was only one organisation working specifically with Scots, as against 20 working for the Irish homeless, backed up by a large pool of directly owned temporary accommodation.

Gaining access to money also proved difficult. Being older than those homeless in Scotland, this group were mainly entitled to full benefit, but it took time to come through, triggering desperate survival problems. In the experience of this group, it took up to four weeks to receive the first GIRO, and the special "No Fixed Abode" Social Security offices seem to release only £2-3 at a time. Almost all had stories about going to "gospel" meetings for free food, hanging around restaurants at closing time, and even stealing. On this basis, shelter was difficult to afford with most London hostels requiring rent up front, and private bedsits requiring both a deposit and the first month's rent in advance.

The average day of the homeless varies according to how recent and successful the arrival in London. Three stories seem to emerge. First, there is the day of the "penniless" new arrival, and the search for money and food. Interestingly, none of this group had begged; they pursued their rights, and in some cases tried to pick up casual work. Second, the day of the search for accommodation. Here any leads are followed up and shared. By now people are street wise and have contacts, and this is described as a better period. Third, as soon as the situation stabilises, comes the day of the serious job hunt.

When the group were asked to consider what they wanted for themselves in the future, there was total agreement. They wanted both,

> *"Decent accommodation and a job."*

That was the spontaneous first response, then someone added,

> *"**Affordable** decent accommodation."*

London was still seen as a better place to find work and build a career if the problem of accommodation costs could be cracked. Only one expressed the desire to return to Scotland, although two were keeping their options open. The most recently arrived was going to give London at least a three month trial. The others planned to stick it out, believing that if you could get through three months you could survive. Finally, to get at least as far as a medium term hostel was seen as a breakthrough.

Taking the advice of young people

This section of the Chapter reports the advice which would be given by those interviewed to young people and to agencies working with homeless groups. The advice given by Scots in London is treated separately due to its specific nature. In sum, these comments can be seen to reflect many of the difficulties experienced when those interviewed became homeless.

Advice is given to those thinking about leaving home and to those who are roofless. Despite the terrible experiences many of these people faced whilst at home – experiences which ultimately drove them away – young people in similar circumstances are warned to be extremely cautious about leaving home. As a result of their own experiences of being roofless, these young people advised,

> *"Try not to leave"* (Sean, 17)

or,

> *"It all depends: if it's a small thing then get them (the young people) to stay in the house"* (Clare, 18)

and again,

> *"Whatever is wrong, try to get it sorted out"* (Stuart, 19).

If the problems at home prove insurmountable, and many expressed an understanding (quite naturally) that this might be the case, then young people are advised to get in contact with helping agencies quickly in order to gain both the accommodation and support needed prior to leaving. The message is to,

> *"Think hard before you leave, and plan"* (Mark, 17)

and then, go to the housing department, The Hamish Allan Centre (run by Glasgow District Council), and the social work department to ask for help. As for contacting social workers these young people conceded that they had needed the help social workers could provide, especially with benefits and accommodation. Social workers were not to be feared, as they themselves had once thought.

The advice to helping agencies was straightforward: they should concentrate on providing more secure accommodation instead of very short term hostels. Four messages emerge. First,

> *"For those who have to leave, they need advice. They need warning as to how difficult homelessness can be."* (Paul, 19)

second,

> *"get them a house."* (Sharon, 17)

third,

> *"We need more facilities, we need more hostels, we need more advice centres!"* (Gary, 18)

and finally, echoing the perception that concern for homeless groups only arises once a year, those interviewed stressed that helping agencies should be aware that,

> *"It (homelessness) is not just happening in the winter, it's happening all year round!"* (Peter, 27).

The London group offered a wide range of ideas, based on three themes, advice to other young Scots, help in Scotland, and help in London. The advice to other young Scots thinking of travelling to London was cautionary in tone, it focused around being adequately prepared and being able to cope upon arrival. The various suggestions included,

> *"Do not attempt to come to London before you are 21."*

> *"Come with a friend, it helps with the culture shock."*

> *"Have some money with you, a lot of money."*

> *"If you are running away, there are better places to run to."*

The advice to agencies in Edinburgh and Glasgow (identified as the main departure points in Scotland), is that they should be prepared to offer counselling to those who are thinking about going down to London. Youngsters should consider ways of setting up accommodation in advance, and if at all possible, employment. Advice should be independent, and not deliberately attempt to dissuade young people from moving South, but rather, offer realistic and constructive help.

The desperate need for facilities to be made available in London for young Scots was mentioned repeatedly. The provision of information packs at arrival points, or a mobile van going round if such permanent service points were a problem, was suggested. In addition, the introduction of "accommodation kiosks" at the main arrival terminals (as for foreign visitors) would be most useful. In total, what is really required is,

"A one-stop shop, a kind of Hamish Allan Centre where money, accommodation, advice and job search could all be sorted out."

Finally, more and better first-stop hostels for young people looking for work should be opened. These hostels should not mix "impressionable" young people with those with drug or alcohol-related problems, or long term itinerants. Obtaining benefit more easily was repeatedly stressed. The Housing Benefit limits seem to hamper job hunts, by making lower paid work uneconomic. These levels need to be changed.

Conclusions

The young people who volunteered to participate in this component of the research project are survivors. Despite their vulnerability and dependency, they have succeeded in gaining access to stable supported accommodation, and can begin to plan for the future. For those who are not so fortunate the future must be bleak. The main findings of this chapter may be summarised as follows:

1 Young people leave home to escape intolerable circumstances. They feel that they are forced to leave as a result of family disputes, often associated with a step-parent. Physical or sexual abuse were also frequently cited. These young people cannot, or at least will not, go home and attempts to make them do so are usually doomed.

2 No one could predict when a family confrontation would force them to leave, and the majority left totally unprepared. Those leaving care had mixed feelings about the quality of the planning process whilst in care, and the after care support available.

3 Attempts to prevent the onset of rooflessness rested in returning home or staying with friends or relatives. For those who became roofless, these arrangements invariably broke down.

4 With extremely limited resources these young people faced immediate survival problems. Many had slept rough, and they all felt extremely lonely. All had difficulty in gaining access to benefits and consequently food. Some were forced through desperation to beg or commit petty offences.

5 Most avoided, or did not know of, the helping agencies that existed. They were afraid, and deeply suspicious, of the social work department, yet in order to cope some contact often proved necessary.

6 The transition from a short stay emergency hostel to more secure accommodation was not straightforward. Often, unsuitable accommodation was offered, or planned moves broke down. When in stable accommodation these young people at last found it possible to prepare for the future.

7 The aspirations held by those interviewed are the same as those held by most people. First, they want to find secure and safe accommodation. Second, they want to get a good job. Unfortunately, many see themselves in "dead end" jobs following on from the Youth Training Scheme. Their greatest fear is to become homeless again.

8 The homeless Scots whom we met in London are older and have more life experiences than those in Scotland. London was positively chosen as a better place to find work. The major problem encountered by this group was finding work which enabled them to afford decent accommodation.

9 All the people interviewed know that they have had a tough time and they urge those responsible to build up services which will make it unnecessary for others to leave home, or ensure that those who leave do not become roofless. The advice offered to young people similarly placed is cautionary. They are warned to think hard and be prepared.

10 While homeless young people are likely to gravitate to the major cities, the problems of poverty, overcrowding, sexual abuse and family disputes which drove them from home are to be found everywhere.

This Chapter has considered the nature of homelessness, and has followed the pathways young people follow both into and out of homelessness, through the words of young people themselves. It has identified the barriers which prevent many young people from successfully moving into an independent living environment. The lessons learned will be carried forward to help in evaluating the ways in which these problems are approached by public services and voluntary agencies.

Part II. Responses

Chapter 3

Young Homeless People And The Law

Introduction

Having outlined the problem we are dealing with in Part I of this Report, we consider the response made to it in Part II. Our first task is to describe the framework of laws which shapes this response, and empowers and constrains those responsible for it. We present this in three main sections: after briefly introducing the agencies involved, we deal first with housing for homeless persons, then with cash benefits, and finally with social work services. In each of these fields we describe the law as briefly and clearly as possible, and then discuss some of the questions which this system poses. Those discussions are drawn together and their policy implications briefly explored in Chapter 7.

General agency framework

Figure 1 outlines the general agency structure for meeting some of the most important needs of young homeless or potentially homeless persons. There are five types of agency involved.

1   The local authority *Housing Department* is mainly concerned with providing accommodation, either through the normal allocation system, or via its duties under the Homeless Persons legislation. The payment of Housing Benefit is also the responsibility of the Housing Authority.

2   The *Department of Social Security* provides several cash benefits which young people may be entitled to including Income Support, Child Benefit and Social Fund payments.

3   The *Department of Employment* is responsible for the payment of Unemployment Benefit and Bridging Allowance. Together with the Careers' Service, it has the task of helping young people find employment and places on training schemes. These schemes include Youth Training for 16 and 17 year olds and Employment Training for persons over 18 who have been unemployed for more than six months.

4   The local authority *Social Work Department* provides support, advice and counselling for young people. It may also help young people living independently to develop 'living skills'. Social workers have an important role in acting as advocates for young people, helping them gain access to resources from the Department of Social Security and the housing department.

Other services like the schools and the NHS, which are also concerned with young people, do not have special responsibilities for those who are, or may become, homeless. Those we have listed are provided by a variety of agencies, both at central and local government level. Many young people have multiple and interacting needs. Clearly we shall have to consider the merits of 'one stop' agencies providing an integrated service to young people, and other methods for bringing together and coordinating the work of different services.

5   Specialist *voluntary agencies* provide a variety of services to young homeless persons. They may receive statutory funding from the social work department under S10(3) of the Social Work (Scotland) Act 1968, or from the housing department under S39 of the Housing (Scotland) Act 1987.

Figure 1. Agency Framework to Meet the Needs of Young Homeless and Potentially Homeless Persons

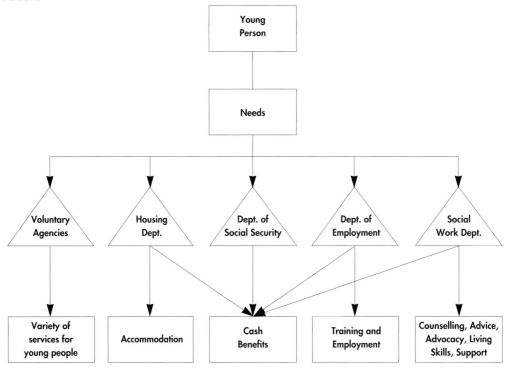

Young People Seeking Accommodation Through The Homeless Persons' Legislation

Introduction

Statutory responsibilities towards the homeless were first placed upon local housing authorities by the Housing (Homeless Persons) Act 1977,[1] and are now contained in Part II of the Housing (Scotland) Act 1987.[2] In carrying out their functions under the Act local authorities must 'have regard' to a Code of Guidance issued by the Secretary of State for Scotland.[3] The Code is not strictly binding on housing authorities, but failure to have regard to its guidance may leave the authority's decision open to challenge by way of judicial review.[4]

Inquiries

If a local authority has 'reason to believe' an applicant may be homeless or 'threatened with homelessness' they are under a duty to make appropriate enquiries.[5] If they also believe he may be in 'priority need' for accommodation they are under an interim duty to secure temporary accommodation pending the outcome of these enquiries.[6] The housing authorities' enquiries concern the key concepts of 'homelessness', 'priority need', 'intentionality', and 'local connection'. We consider these in turn.

Homelessness

An applicant is 'homeless' if he has no accommodation in Great Britain which he (together with his partner or family) is entitled to occupy.[7] Statute provides that a person is not to be treated as having accommodation unless it is reasonable for him to continue to occupy it (taking into account the prevailing housing circumstances of the area).[8]

The courts have held that temporary or crisis accommodation does not constitute accommodation for the purposes of the Homeless Persons' legislation.[9]

A person who has accommodation may nevertheless be homeless if he cannot gain entry to it,[10] or occupation would lead to violence or threats of violence likely to be carried out from another resident,[11] or it is overcrowded *and* a danger to health.[12]

A person is 'threatened with homelessness' if he is likely to become homeless within 28 days.[13]

If the local authority find the applicant is *not* 'homeless', or 'threatened with homelessness' they must provide reasons for their decision, but have no further duty.[14]

Priority Need

To qualify for accommodation a person must not only be homeless but must also have a 'priority need' for accommodation. Young homeless persons are not among those specified by the legislation as having a 'priority need', but they may be included in the general category of those who are 'vulnerable' for some 'other special reason' and consequently have a priority need for accommodation.[15]

The Code of Guidance advises that 16 and 17 year olds will often be at risk from sexual or financial exploitation if they have left home without moving to secure accommodation, and if so should be treated as vulnerable,[16] as should young people over 17 who are at risk from similar exploitation because of the circumstance in which they are living.[17] The Code also advises that young people who have recently left local authority care may be considered vulnerable if they have no one to support and assist them.[18] The Code of Guidance recommends that the housing authority should where appropriate co-operate with social work departments in assessing vulnerability.[19]

Local authorities must have regard to the above guidance, but are not obliged to follow it. The Code of Guidance itself stresses that these are only examples of persons who may be vulnerable for some 'other special reason'; and sympathetic judgement and common sense should be exercised in the circumstances of each individual case.[20] Recent research has shown that, in practice, local authorities place widely differing interpretations on the 'priority need' of young, homeless people.[21] In particular, only 15% of local authorities automatically class young people leaving care as priority cases (although 80% do so sometimes),[22] and 35% of local authorities at least sometimes define young single people as having a 'priority need' on the basis of age alone, half of these classifying them as such automatically.[23]

Two important but contrasting cases should be noted in the context of the 'priority need' of very young homeless people. In *Kelly v. Monklands DC*[24] Lord Ross, whilst affirming that not every 16 year old girl was vulnerable within the meaning of the legislation, held that youth in combination with other factors such as lack of income and family support did raise a *prima facie* case of priority need which may be difficult to rebut. However, in *Steventon v. Monklands DC*[25] it was held that the local authority were entitled to find a 16 year old boy was not 'vulnerable', despite social work advice to the contrary. So long as they had regard to this advice, they were free to depart from it on the basis of their own evidence and judgement.

If a local authority find that an applicant who is homeless or threatened with homelessness is *not* in 'priority need' their duty is limited to providing appropriate advice and assistance to enable the applicant to retain or secure accommodation for himself or herself.[26]

Intentionality

If a local authority find an applicant is homeless and in 'priority need', they must then consider whether he became homeless *intentionally*. In this regard the onus is on the local authority to establish that the applicant deliberately did or failed to do something in consequence of which he lost accommodation which was available for his occupation and which it would have been reasonable for him to continue to occupy.[27]

The Code gives guidance on the meaning of '*deliberate*' in the context of some common cases of homelessness, e.g. wilful and persistent refusal to pay rent can be considered intentional, but not rent arrears because of real personal or financial difficulties.[28] It is provided by the legislation that an act or omission on the part of the applicant where he is unaware of some relevant fact is not to be regarded as deliberate, e.g. if the claimant runs up rent arrears because he is unaware of his entitlement to Housing Benefit.[29]

It must have been *reasonable* for the applicant to continue to occupy the accommodation which was available to him. A person should not be treated as intentionally homeless if he could not reasonably have been expected to remain in the accommodation because of, e.g. overcrowding, lack of basic facilities or severe emotional stress.[30] However, the legislation provides that regard may be had to the general housing circumstances of the area in determining whether it would be reasonable for a person to continue to occupy accommodation.[31] The Code of Guidance is clear that victims of domestic violence and young people who have left home because of physical or sexual abuse should never be considered intentionally homeless.[32]

One of the prime considerations regarding intentionality should be the immediate cause of homelessness and not events which took place previously,[33] and findings of intentional homelessness should be subject to review if there is a change in the circumstances of the applicant.[34]

An applicant is *intentionally threatened* with homelessness "if he deliberately does or fails to do anything the likely result of which is that he will be forced to leave accommodation which is available for his occupation and which it would have been reasonable for him to continue to occupy".[35]

If a local authority deem an applicant to be intentionally homeless their duty is limited to providing temporary accommodation and appropriate advice and assistance.[36] If they are intentionally 'threatened with homelessness' the local authority must provide advice and assistance only.[37]

Local connection

If a local authority find an applicant to be unintentionally homeless and in priority need, they have a discretionary power to investigate whether the applicant has a *'local connection'* with the area of another local authority.[38] This can arise through normal residence, employment, family association or other special circumstances.[39]

If the applicant has no local connection with the authority to whom the application was made, and has a local connection with another local authority where he or she runs no risk of domestic violence, then the local authority may transfer responsibility for the permanent rehousing of the applicant to that other authority.[40]

Summary

If a young person can establish that he is *homeless*, in *priority need* for accommodation, and is *not intentionally homeless*, the local authority must ensure that *permanent accommodation* is available for him (unless they can transfer that responsibility under the *local connection* rules).[41] This does not have to be, but normally is, a council tenancy.

If a young person can establish that he is *unintentionally 'threatened with homelessness'*, and is in *priority need* for accommodation, then the local authority must *take reasonable steps* to ensure that the accommodation he has *does not cease to be available to him*.[42]

Remedies

If a local authority reaches an adverse decision on any of the four issues of 'homelessness', 'priority need', 'intentionality' and 'local connection' they must inform the applicant of the reasons for their decision.[43] However, there is no statutory appeal either to the courts or to the Secretary of State from the decisions of local authorities on homelessness applications. The applicant must either seek a political solution through his local councillor, or if he feels he has suffered injustice as a result of 'maladministration' on the part of the local authority he can complain to the Local Authority Ombudsman.

Alternatively, the applicant may challenge the legality of the decision by way of judicial review in the Court of Session. Judicial review is the means by which the courts ensure that administrative decisions of public authorities are taken according to law. The basic tenets of judicial review are that public authorities must not exceed or misuse administrative powers, and they must conform to certain basic principles of procedural fairness. However judicial review is not an appeal on the merits of a decision, but simply an examination of its legality. So long as local authorities act within the bounds of legality the Court will not interfere with their decisions. Specific grounds on which the Court of Session will invalidate housing authority decisions include misinterpretation of the law; failing to take into account relevant considerations or failing to disregard irrelevant considerations;[44] manifest unreasonableness;[45] fettering of discretion; and unfair procedure.[46]

The form of proceeding is called an 'application for judicial review', and is a simplified and expedited procedure as a result of reforms in 1985. Legal Aid (including Emergency Legal Aid) and Legal Advice and Assistance are both available for judicial review actions to those persons with sufficiently low income and capital. This will include most homeless young people.[47]

The Code of Guidance recommends that local authorities should consider setting up internal appeals systems for homeless applicants, but many have yet to establish an effective appeals procedure.[48]

Discussion

There are many barriers a young person must negotiate in order to secure permanent accommodation through the Homeless Persons' legislation. Local authorities have discretion at many stages in this process to either interpret their duties generously in favour of, or restrictively against, the homeless applicant. Particularly relevant to young single people is the wide discretion involved in assessing 'vulnerability' for the purposes of the 'priority need' qualification. The depletion of council housing stock in the last decade, particularly through the 'Right to Buy' legislation, must inevitably bring pressure on local authorities to interpret their responsibilities more and more strictly in order to limit the number of homeless applicants they have to rehouse.

With their own housing resources greatly diminished, many local authorities have established nomination procedures with housing associations and other bodies to help them fulfil their obligation to secure permanent accommodation for homeless persons in priority need. However, the housing resources made available to local authorities by these means are unlikely to compensate for the reduction in their own housing stock, thus homeless persons are likely to face increasing difficulties in securing accommodation through the homeless persons' legislation – particularly in view of the growing numbers of single person households on the councils' waiting lists for housing. Young homeless persons as a low priority group are likely to experience the greatest difficulties in securing accommodation, whether as homeless persons or via normal allocation procedures.

These problems are exacerbated by the lack of an effective remedy for homeless people to enforce what rights they do possess under this legislation. The remedies presently available are generally narrow in scope (judicial review and Ombudsman); slow (Ombudsman); expensive (judicial review); or unreliable (political solutions). Under the National Health Service and Community Care Act of 1990, social work departments are required to set up procedures for dealing with complaints but it is too early to assess how well these work. The other remedies are undoubtedly valuable to the limited number of homeless persons who are able to use them, but what is needed for the great bulk of homeless people is a clearly accessible, cheap and swift means of enforcing their legal rights. Such a facility is granted to almost all other groups granted rights in law.

Accessing Accommodation Through The Homeless Persons' Legislation

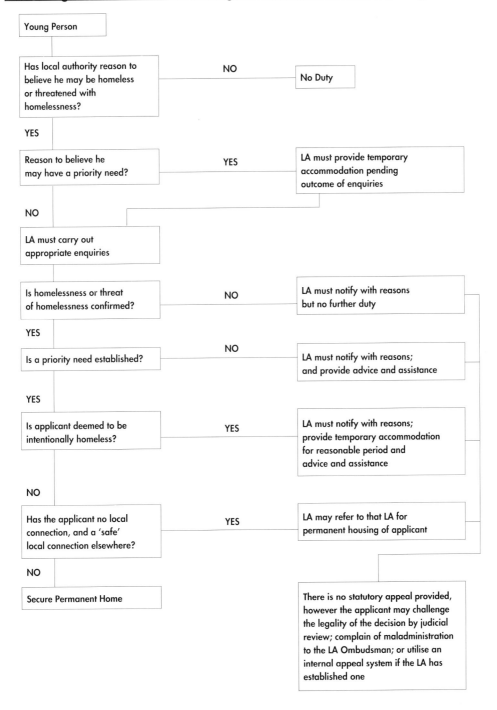

Note: Based on Scottish Code of Guidance Diagram: 'Assessing Homeless Applications'.

Cash Benefits To Young People

Introduction

Changes in the social security and tax system in recent years have often been unfavourable to young single people and childless couples. There are now three distinct age bands governing young people's access to benefits: 16 and 17 year olds; 18-24 year olds; and those aged 25 or over. Changes to the social security system have had particularly serious consequences for young people aged 16 and 17.

Unemployment Benefit

This is a contributory benefit paid by the Department of Employment to unemployed persons who are 'available for' and 'actively seeking' employment.[49] Claimants who are deemed 'voluntarily unemployed' by the legislation will be disqualified from Unemployment Benefit (UB) for up to 26 weeks.[50] UB is payable for 52 weeks at a rate of £43.10 to those with the necessary contributions record.

Contribution conditions were made significantly more onerous in 1988. The claimant must have *actually paid* Class I contributions producing an earnings factor at least 25 times that year's lower earnings limit in one of the last two complete tax years before the benefit year in which UB is claimed. He must also have either paid or been credited with contributions producing an earnings factor of 50 times the lower earnings limit in *each* of the last two complete contribution years before the relevant benefit year.[51]

These contribution conditions mean that it is only those 18 or over with a good work record who may be entitled to UB. We found that most of the young homeless are under the age of 20 and have, at best, intermittent work records. Thus most of the people whom this study is concerned with are effectively excluded from unemployment benefit.

Income Support

Income Support (IS) replaced supplementary benefit in 1988 as the main non-contributory benefit for people on low incomes.[52]

To qualify for IS the claimant – or "customer" as they are now called – must be 18 or over;[53] must not be in full-time paid employment[54] or receiving full-time education;[55] must be 'available for' and 'actively seeking' employment;[56] and his income[57] and capital[58] must be below a prescribed amount. The maximum capital threshold is currently £8,000.[59].

The customer's income must be below the 'applicable amount'. This is an amount set by law as necessary for living expenses depending on the claimant's personal circumstances. The 'applicable amount' is comprised of 'personal allowances'; 'premiums' for special needs; and 'housing costs' to cover certain costs of accommodation not met by Housing Benefit e.g. mortgage interest payments.[60]

Benefit is calculated by deducting the customer's income from his applicable amount.[61]

The current personal allowance for single customers aged 18-24 is £33.60, and aged 25 and over is £42.25. For couples where one or both partners are 18 or over the current personal allowance is £66.60.[62]

Until 1988 16 and 17 year olds were entitled to benefit under the same conditions as customers aged 18 or over. However, now to be eligible for IS young people under 18 must either satisfy prescribed conditions in the IS regulations,[63] or be the subject of a direction by the Secretary of State for Social Security that severe hardship will occur unless IS is paid.[64]

Under the regulations some 16 and 17 year olds are entitled to IS until they are 18 (so long as they satisfy the other entitlement conditions). This mainly relates to young people who are sick or disabled, pregnant, lone parents, full-time carers, etc.[65] Some 16 and 17 year olds are entitled to IS during the Child Benefit extension period, including young people who are living away from their parents because of physical or sexual abuse.[66]

The decisions on severe hardship are actually made by the Severe Hardship Claims Unit in Glasgow. They normally take several weeks to deliver any benefit which may then continue only for a few weeks. The test is strict, as it must be established that *severe* hardship *will* (not may) result if IS is not paid. As it is technically the decision of the Secretary of State for Social Security there is no appeal to the normal adjudicating authorities. Severe hardship payment may be made for any period the Secretary of State determines,[67] and may be revoked on any change of circumstances which means that severe hardship will no longer necessarily result from non-payment of IS.[68] The customer will lose entitlement if he or she ceases to satisfy any of the other conditions of entitlement to IS.

The current personal allowance for single customers under 18 is £25.55, and for couples when both are under 18 is £50.60.[69]

For the single youngsters this study is concerned with the IS offered to those suffering recognised severe hardship is only 61% of that paid to people over 25. That also reduces their Housing Benefit, as we explain below.

Bridging Allowance

This was introduced in 1988 when 16 and 17 year olds became disentitled from Income Support.[70]

It is paid at the discretion of the Secretary of State for Employment to 16 and 17 year olds who are moving from one training scheme to another or from a job to training, and are not entitled to IS or UB.[71]

It is payable at a rate of £15 per week, for up to 8 weeks in a 52 week period. It may be stopped if the young person refuses *any* offer of a YT place and, as with the 'voluntarily unemployed' disqualification from UB, the young person can be disqualified for up to 26 weeks.

Extended Child Benefit

Extended Child Benefit was introduced in 1988 for 16 and 17 year olds who have left school, been unable to find employment and are not receiving IS. To qualify the young person must be registered as available for work or training.[72]

The parents or guardians of the young person can claim child benefit for three or four months after the young person has left school (depending on school leaving date).[73] It is currently payable at a rate of £9.65 for the only or eldest child, and £7.80 for each subsequent child.[74]

Housing Benefit

If young people live independently and are responsible for paying rent they may be able to claim Housing Benefit. To qualify the claimant must have capital of £16,000 or less; their income must be low enough (see below); and he or she must not come under a specific exclusion – e.g. full-time students are excluded.[74]

Entitlement is concerned with the concept of Maximum Housing Benefit (MHB). This equals 100% of eligible rent, less any deductions for non-dependants.

Normally a customer's full rent is eligible but some payments are excluded, e.g. charges for fuel and water rates;[75] and from April 1991 the local authority *must* consider whether or not accommodation is unsuitable because it is too large or expensive, in which case it must reduce rent to a figure which it thinks appropriate in relation to suitable alternative accommodation.[76] The 'rent stop' does not operate for the first 13 weeks of a claim if when you moved into the accommodation you were able to meet the housing cost, unless you have claimed HB within 52 weeks of your current benefit period.[77]

A deduction may be made from HB if a 'non-dependant' lives with the customer.[78] The legislation is intended to ensure that such persons contribute to the housing costs of the household. 'Non-dependants' include adult sons and daughters,[79] and so can lead to additional pressures in families trying to survive on low incomes. The present 'non-dependant' deductions are: £18, £12, £8, £4 and nil, depending on the employment status and income of the non-dependant.[80] Among those exempted from being 'non-dependants' are the under 18s, under 25s on IS and students.

If a customer receives IS or his income is below the 'applicable amount' (calculated as for IS except without the housing cost element) he receives MHB.[81] If his income is more than the 'applicable amount' his MHB is reduced by 65% of the difference between his income and the applicable amount.[82]

Benefit = MHB – 65% (Income-Applicable Amount)

This sharp taper means that the cut-off point for HB is quite low, and 18-24 year olds receive a lower rate than over 25s because the 'personal allowance' element of their applicable amount is lower (as in IS). It should be noted that 16 and 17 year olds *are* eligible for HB, but similarly their rate of HB is lower because their 'personal allowances' are lower.

Social Fund

The Social Fund replaced in 1988 the single payments and urgent needs payments previously payable under the Supplementary Benefits Scheme.[83] The discretionary Social Fund contains the following categories of payment which may be available to young people; Crisis Loans, Budget Loans and Community Care Grants. Crisis Loans and Budget Loans are *repayable*,[84] usually by deductions in future benefit. Community Care Grants (CCG) are non-repayable, but like Crisis and Budget Loans are paid on a *discretionary basis*.[85] The Social Fund is *budget limited*; there is an allocation of a separate cash limit for loans and for grants for each Benefits Agency District.[86] Social Fund Offices (SFOs) cannot make payments from the Fund which would cause the budget allocation for that year to be exceeded.[87] Therefore it is important for applicants to establish themselves as having a high priority need to receive payment under the discretionary Social Fund. Guidance from the Secretary of State for Social Security in the Social Fund Manual sets out general illustrations of high, medium and low priority needs and groups of applicants, and within Districts, managers similarly set out priorities in local guidance. The local budget is managed according to these priorities,[88] but SFOs must examine the particular circumstances of each individual case in determining whether or not to make a Social Fund payment.[89]

Community Care Grants are available only to people receiving IS who either are trying to re-establish themselves in the community after a period in institutional care, or to help an individual remain in the community rather than go into institutional care.[90] Young people leaving care, or young people estranged from their parents are among the priority groups for CCG in the Secretary of State for Social Security's guidance.[91] It is a non-repayable grant, but any kind of housing costs are excluded.[92]

Budgeting loans are only available to applicants who have been receiving IS for at least 26 weeks.[93] They are intended to cover important intermittent expenses for which the applicant is unable to budget.[94] The SFO must take into account your ability to repay a Budget (or Crisis) Loan.[95] Paradoxically this means that those on the lowest incomes are likely to be refused a Social Fund payment. Budgeting Loans are not available for most housing costs including deposits for accommodation or residential charges for hostels.[96] Rent in advance is permissible.

Crisis Loans are available to persons who do not have sufficient resources to meet their immediate short term needs,[97] and the loan is only available to meet expenses in an emergency or as a consequence of a disaster. A Crisis Loan must be the only way to avoid serious damage or risk to your health and safety;[98] or be for rent in advance to a private landlord.[99] Crisis Loans are not available for most other housing costs.[100] 16 and 17 year olds *are* eligible for Crisis Loans as the applicant does not have to be receiving IS.

Community Charge and Community Charge Benefit

In April 1989 domestic rates were replaced by three 'community charges'.[101] Only the 'personal' and 'collective' community charges are relevant for our purposes. The personal community charge is, with very few exceptions, payable by all adult (18 or over) residents in a local authority area. The collective community charge is payable by persons 18 or over who reside in short term accommodation, e.g. hostels and refuges.

The principle underlying the community charge is that all adults should contribute to the cost of local authority services on a flat rate basis. However there is a Community Charge Benefit (CCB) scheme to help those on the lowest incomes pay their community charge. The maximum CCB is 80% of your community charge.[102] Persons entitled to IS or whose income is lower than their 'applicable amount' for IS purposes will receive maximum CCB.[103] Persons whose income is higher than their 'applicable amount' receive maximum CCB less 15% of the difference between their income and their 'applicable amount'.[104]

Benefit = Maximum CCB – 15% (Income – 'applicable amount')

It should be noted, therefore, that almost all adults have to pay at least 20% of their community charge.

Discussion

Young people need sufficient income if they are to sustain tenancies and generally make a success of independent living. It must be accepted that despite Government policy, many young people continue to choose, or are forced, to leave home before they are 25, some before they are 18. Many of these young people are unemployed or on low wages, so are dependent on state benefits to maintain their income at an adequate level to provide themselves with accommodation and the other basic essentials of life.

Recent benefit changes have made it much more difficult than it was before 1988 for many young people to maintain an adequate level of income. Those in the 18-24 year old age group receive a lower rate of IS and HB than those aged 25 or over. This causes great difficulties for young people who are trying to establish or maintain independent households on very low incomes. This age group also has the added burden of paying at least 20% of their local authority community charge. This further reduction in the disposable income of the over 18s increases hardship for many young people who have left home. The increased burden the community charge places on the overall household budget of families with young people aged 18 or over may well create an intolerable strain on some low income households, perhaps precipitating the ejection and future homelessness of young people from these households. The property based 'Council Tax' due to come into force in April 1993 may alleviate some of these problems.

The problems faced by 16 and 17 year olds who have left home and have no or little income are even more serious. Generally speaking, they are not entitled to IS, and the severe hardships provisions, Bridging Allowance and extension of Child Benefit provide a very incomplete safety net for this age group. Many 16 and 17 year olds are suffering hardship as a result, and some are completely destitute with no income at all. In these circumstances it is impossible for them to make a successful transition to independent living. Even when benefits are paid to them, these may take many weeks to deliver.

Young people trying to set up home often need lump sums of money to pay for deposits for accommodation, furniture and equipment for their homes, and rent in advance to private landlords. Young people trying to secure payment from the Social Fund for these purposes will encounter various difficulties. The first of these being eligibility for payment. Community Care Grant and Budgeting Loan are only available to persons receiving IS, so most 16 and 17 year olds are completely excluded. Community Care Grants are only available to those with an 'institutional care' background, and Crisis Loans are only payable in very tightly drawn circumstances. Even when payments are made they may take a long time to arrive – sometimes compelling young people to pay rent for flats which they cannot live in owing to lack of basic furniture.

Even those young people who are eligible for a Social Fund payment may not receive it unless they can establish that they have a high priority need, because the Fund is discretionary and budget limited. Even the most deserving case cannot receive payment if this would mean the local budget being exceeded. Both the Crisis and Budgeting Loans are repayable, and the ability of a young person to repay any loan will be taken into account when deciding whether or not to grant it. Some young people on very low incomes will therefore be denied lump sums which they need, but are unable to repay.

The final problem for young people trying to get money from the Social Fund to secure or maintain accommodation is that housing costs such as deposits for flats or residential charges for hostels are excluded items from Crisis Loans or Budgeting Loans, and housing costs of any kind are excluded from Community Care Grants.

For young people to avoid homelessness they must be able to secure accommodation, and they often need rent in advance or deposits in order to do so. For the tenancies to be successful they must be able to furnish and equip their new homes. The Social Fund fails to provide the help necessary in terms of cash lump sums which many young people need to set up home successfully. That and other reductions in benefit were deliberate policy decisions taken by Parliament in 1988.

Cash Benefits Available To Young People

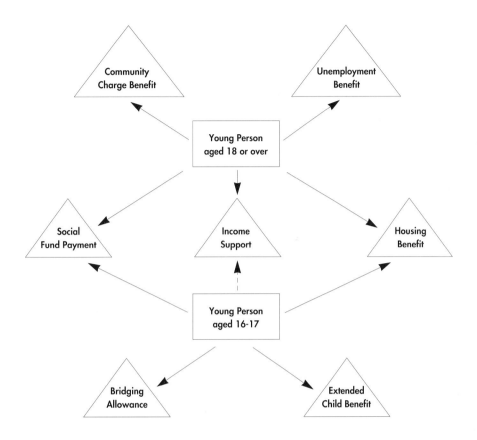

Social Work Responsibilities
To Young People

Introduction

The Social Work (Scotland) Act 1968 provides the main legislative framework within which social work authorities currently operate. This legislation was framed at a time in which there were very few homeless young people, consequently social work responsibilities towards this group are not well defined in law.

Social work law is, however, in a state of flux at the moment regarding both child and adult care. The NHS and Community Care Act 1990 has implications for adult care in England, Wales and Scotland, and the Children's Act 1989 fundamentally alters child law in England and Wales. The Child Care Law Review published in December 1990, is likely to be the subject of a White Paper later in the year, and has made important recommendations for changes to child care law in Scotland.

These developments contain policy approaches and specific provisions which may be of interest in the context of social work responsibilities to young homeless or potentially homeless persons.

Four main areas of social work responsibilities can be identified as of relevance to young homeless or potentially homeless persons. Social work authorities have certain duties regarding homeless persons generally; they have a general duty to promote social welfare in the community; social work has particular responsibilities towards children who are in, or have previously been in, local authority care; and duties are placed on social work authorities regarding specific client groups to whom some homeless young people may belong.

Social work duties to homeless persons

Social work authorities do have some specific duties as regards homeless persons, but these are contained within housing, rather than social work legislation. S38 of the Housing (Scotland) Act 1987 places a duty on social work authorities to render whatever assistance is reasonable in the circumstances if requested by a housing authority to help it discharge its functions under the homeless persons' legislation, or to exercise any of its functions in respect of a particular case.

The Code of Guidance to the homeless persons' legislation encourages co-operation between social work and housing authorities to help divert the threat of homelessness. It recommends the establishment of formal liaison arrangement between the social work and housing authorities,[105] and the arrangement of joint meetings and training programmes for their officers, in order to facilitate this co-operation.[106] The Code also describes various areas in which the co-operation of social work with housing authorities will be particularly useful in the prevention or alleviation of homelessness.[107] The Code is, however, only guidance and is not binding on social work or housing authorities.

The present legislation does, therefore, place some responsibility for homeless persons on social work authorities, but these are duties owed to housing authorities dealing with homelessness rather than to homeless persons themselves. In any case the duties are too limited and vague to be of much value in establishing a statutory right for homeless persons to receive help from social work authorities.

General duty of social work authorities to promote social welfare

S12 of the Social Work (Scotland) Act 1968 places a general *duty* on social work authorities to promote social welfare by providing advice, guidance and assistance on an appropriate scale for their area.

Social work departments provide varying degrees of advice and guidance to young homeless persons, and are often very important as advocates for such young people, helping them gain access to resources from other agencies such as housing departments and the DSS.

More specifically under S12, social work authorities have *power* to promote assistance in kind, or in exceptional circumstances in cash, to children under the age of 18, if such assistance is likely to diminish the need to receive the child into, or keep him in, local authority care.[108]

Similarly assistance may be provided in kind, or in exceptional circumstances, constituting an emergency, in cash, to a "person in need" where this will avoid the local authority greater expense on a later occasion.[109] A "person in need" includes those requiring care and attention arising out of "youth",[110] however, this was not originally intended to cover young people other than those previously in care.

Social work authorities have felt themselves to be under increasing pressure to provide financial assistance through S12 funds because of the social security changes restricting benefits for young people, particularly 16 and 17 year olds. However, it is unclear to what extent young homeless or potentially homeless persons are considered 'persons in need' for the purpose of this provision.

The Child Care Law Review has recommended that although there should be no transfer of income maintenance responsibility from central to local government, there should be a widening of the scope of S12 to give explicit entitlement to assistance to all young people under 18 to promote their welfare in the community.[111] They also recommend that a Code of Practice be introduced, illustrating a range of support services to be provided by social work authorities, with special reference to the needs of the 16 to 18 year old age group.[112]

Responsibilities to young people with a 'care' background

There are a number of routes through which children come into local authority care. Children may be in 'voluntary care' under S15 of the 1968 Act, which places a duty upon local authorities to provide for children under the age of 17 who are lost, abandoned, have no parents or guardians, or whose parents or guardians fail to properly provide for them. Children may be in voluntary care so long as their welfare requires it and they have not reached 18.

Children may be subject to compulsory measures of care ordered by the Children's Hearing under Section 44 of the 1968 Act. The Hearing may make a supervision requirement requiring the child to submit to supervision at home, away from home with relatives or foster parents, or in residential accommodation. In these cases the child is in the care of the local authority only for the purposes of certain specified sections,[113] including those relating to after-care. Supervision requirements are terminated by the Children's Hearing, a Sheriff, or the child reaching 18 years of age, or where no review of the requirement has been made within a period of one year of the making of the requirement.

Children may also come into care through the Matrimonial Proceedings (Scotland) Act 1958,[114] the Adoption (Scotland) Act 1978[115] and the Guardianship Act 1973.[116]

Certain legal consequences flow from the status of a child as being 'in care'. The local authority has a duty to safeguard and promote the welfare of any child in its care,[117] to review his or her case regularly,[118] and the local authority has certain aftercare responsibilities to children previously 'in care'.

The 'aftercare' responsibilities of social work authorities are contained in S24 and S26 of the 1968 Act.

S24 *empowers* local authorities to contribute to the cost of accommodation and maintenance of young people over school age and under 21, so long as they are in, or have been in, the care of a local authority *after* ceasing to be of school age. The local authority can also make grants to these young people to enable them to pursue suitable education or training.

S26 imposes a *duty* on local authorities to provide advice, guidance and assistance to young people under 18 who left care on or after school leaving date, unless the local authority is satisfied that the welfare of the young person does not require it.

It is widely recognised that young people need a great deal of support, emotionally and materially, to make a successful transition to independent living. Such support is often not available to young people leaving care, and the particular vulnerabilities of this group, (many of whom have serious social or personal problems, are very young when they choose to live independently, and may have been institutionalised by long periods in residential care) make effective aftercare support essential if these young people are to avoid homelessness and poverty.

However, the aftercare provisions outlined above are very limited. They are restricted to those young people who were in care at or after school leaving age, excluding many young people who spend a considerable amount of time in care, but leave shortly before they are 16. Furthermore S26 only applies to young people under 18, and in any case allows a great deal of discretion to local authorities in deciding the content of this assistance. S24 help is available till a young person is 21, but this is only a power not a duty, and it is to be expected that local authorities will vary greatly in the level of assistance, if any, which they provide under this section.

The Child Care Law Review has made a number of proposals for reform to strengthen the aftercare services available to young people. They recommend that local authorities should have a duty to provide advice and assistance to any young person over school leaving age who has spent a significant part of his or her life in care since the age of 12, whenever the young person requests it and the local authority agree that their needs require it. This aftercare should be available till the young person reaches 21.[119] The Review recommends that local authorities be required to establish a range of services to offer to young people who have been in care.[120]

They also propose that local authorities be placed under a new duty to prepare children for leaving care, whether this be a return to the family home or a move towards independent living.[121]

Under the Children's Act 1989 local authorities in England and Wales have powers to provide accommodation for young people up to the age of 21, even if they have not previously been in local authority care.[122] Therefore 'aftercare' in England extends much further than the present position in Scotland, or indeed the Child Care Law Review recommendations. However this is, at least partly, a reflection of the differing legal status of young people in England and Scotland from the age of 16. Scottish 16 and 17 year olds have traditionally had more rights to live independently, get married without parental consent, enter tenancy agreements etc., so it may not be entirely appropriate to apply the english model in the scottish context.

Social work responsibilities to specific client groups

There are several specific client groups in respect of whom social work authorities have particular powers and duties. Young homeless or potentially homeless persons form part of some of these groups.

S27 of the 1968 Act places a duty on social work authorities to provide advice, guidance and assistance to persons on probation or released from prison and on probation. S27B gives power to the Secretary of State to make grants to local authorities to provide hostel accommodation for persons on probation.

"Persons in need" under S12 of the 1968 Act are, as mentioned above, entitled to advice, guidance and assistance from the social work authority, including assistance in kind or in cash in some circumstances. Those defined as persons in need who may also be young and homeless, or potentially homeless, include the mentally ill, mentally handicapped, persons suffering from illness or substantially handicapped by disability or deformity.

The NHS and Community Care Act 1990 places new responsibilities on social work authorities in respect of those to whom they provide 'community care services'. This includes services, other than services provided to children, which social work authorities provide under S12 of the 1968 Act (above), the provision of residential care under S12, the provision of home help services under S14 of the Act, and services to those with a mental disorder under the Mental Health (Scotland) Act 1984.[123]

From April 1992 social work authorities will have to prepare a 'community care plan' for the provision of these services over a three year period, and update it annually.[124] In preparing these plans social work authorities must consult the Health Board in their area, the housing authority if the plan has implications for housing, and relevant voluntary organisations. The other important new duty is concerned with the assessment of needs of persons to whom they have community care responsibilities.[125] Having identified a person as possibly in need of community care services, the social work authority must carry out a full assessment of that person's needs. They must then consider whether the person has the means to provide for his or her needs independently, and if not whether the local authority should provide those services taking into account available resources and how the person's needs rank in comparison with competing priorities.

The legislation is widely drawn but the White Paper preceding it indicated that community care primarily concerned the mentally ill, mentally handicapped, ageing and physically or sensorily disabled.[126] It is unclear if young homeless people, as a group, have any place in the community care framework, although individual young people will clearly be included if they come into any of the above categories.

Discussion

The legal structure of social work responsibilities to young homeless people shows the marks of two major changes which have taken place since the 1968 Act was formulated. Firstly, the transfer of responsibilities for homeless people from social work and welfare agencies to housing authorities has left social work with continuing but ill-defined powers and few firm duties in this field. Secondly, the recent and dramatic rise in the numbers of young homeless people is a development for which neither the services nor the legislation were prepared.

Social work responsibilities must be clarified and strengthened if there is to be a firm legal basis for social work services to play any role in the prevention and management of youth homelessness. Presently the vagueness of responsibilities to young homeless people is allowing them to become a fairly low priority in the heavy caseloads of professional social workers.

A clear inclusion of vulnerable young homeless or potentially homeless people in the 'Community Care' programme would encourage this clarification of responsibilities between the two key agencies – Housing and Social Work – and would give young people rights to assessment and the resources available to help vulnerable groups in the 'Community Care' programme. The resource implications arising from young people's inclusion in the community care framework may be more than recouped in the longer term, as these young people are likely to make less demands on public services if properly supported at this crucial stage in their transition to independent living and adulthood.

Also relevant in this context is the Child Care Law Review's recommendations regarding widening the scope of financial and other assistance under S12 to under 18s. If implemented these could provide a very valuable support to vulnerable 16 and 17 year olds, and particularly if the proposed Code of Practice is introduced with clear illustrations of the types of services most helpful to the 16 to 18 year old age group.

Among the most vulnerable young people are those leaving local authority care, many of whom are in urgent need of social work support in lieu of the family support which other young people can rely on. In this regard the Child Care Law Review has made important recommendations for the strengthening of the aftercare services available to such young people, and has proposed that local authorities be under a new duty to prepare young people to cope with their lives after leaving care.

In the light of repeated evidence that care leavers form a disproportionate part of the overall young homeless population, these proposals to strengthen and extend local authority duties of 'aftercare' seem eminently sensible and long overdue.

There seems a particularly strong case for the inclusion of young people leaving care in the 'Community Care' programme. This follows not only from the specific needs and vulnerabilities of this group, but also from the ethos of community care – i.e. its purpose of helping those with an institutional care background to make a successful transition to living in the community. In view of this, the failure to include young people leaving local authority care in the 'Community Care' programme is clearly anomalous.

The needs of homeless young people have emerged as a result of economic and social changes which were not foreseen, and policy changes which were based on a misunderstanding of these trends. It is not surprising that the law affecting housing, social security services and social work for these young people needs amendment at many points. We explore this legal agenda in Chapter 7. But first we must show how these services actually work.

Notes to this Chapter appear as Appendix 1 to our Report.

Chapter 4

Agency Response To Homeless Applications: Evidence Drawn From The Vignette Data Analysis

Introduction

We have described the legal framework supporting – and constraining – society's response to the needs of homeless young people. But how does this system actually work? We answer that question in two ways. First, in this Chapter, we report how staff of selected services, representing the main agencies dealing with homeless youngsters, said they would respond to four imaginary but typical cases. Then, in the next Chapter, we report how the same agencies actually dealt with young homeless people.

In effect, we used these different methods to make case studies of nine agencies. In each of the nine case study locations four homeless persons' vignettes were presented to workers as examples of potential clients. The interviewees were asked to interpret the vignettes and identify their agency's likely response to each application for assistance. Employing this analysis of data elicited by vignettes, we were able to explore the complex nature of the assessment process and gain insight into the type of service young homeless people are likely to receive in different settings. In total, 75 interviews were held for each vignette. This Chapter presents the findings of this exercise and draws conclusions from them.

First, a brief explanation of vignette data analysis, its purpose and design, will be given. Second, the agencies which participated in the research will be classified according to type and setting. Third, we explain who was interviewed. Fourth, the information collected will be explained. Fifth, the findings relating to each vignette will be explored, and complemented with evidence drawn from a similar study which we made of Perth and Kinross District in 1991. Finally, a series of conclusions will be presented.

Vignette data analysis: purpose and design

The research technique of vignette data analysis has several advantages. First, the agencies which participated in the research programme were located in various settings and dealt with different kinds of clients. Employing vignettes enabled a standardised evaluation of the nature of agency responses to be made. Second, this technique creates an environment similar to that of emergency presentations. The analysis of 'live' cases which we present in the next Chapter does not identify all the factors which make effective case management so difficult. Employing vignettes enables some judgement to be made about the barriers to long term intervention, and provides an important insight into the type of help offered to young people who never become a "case". Research conducted in live situations is time consuming and does not provide uniform, comparable data. In addition, the researcher is placed in an extremely sensitive situation which might damage their own and the agencies' work.

Vignettes provide the interviewee with a limited amount of data about potential clients. In order to interpret these accounts, the interviewee is required to draw upon their experience of working with similar applicants. The vignettes were constructed with the assistance of experienced practitioners – in particular, area team social workers. Together they were agreed to be "typical" of many groups of young people who present themselves as homeless.

The case study agencies

The agencies which participated in the research programme were located in Strathclyde and Lothian regions. The nature of these agencies, including both function and setting, can be outlined as follows:

(a) Of the five agencies which were located in Strathclyde region, two were social work area teams, two were specialist social work agencies working with young people and homeless young people, and one was a district council housing office.

(b) Of the four agencies which were located in Lothian region, two were social work area teams, one was a specialist social work team, and one was a specialist voluntary organisation funded in part by the regional council social work department.

For clarity of presentation, these agencies have been labelled as follows:

Social work area team – Lothian	(A)
Social work area team – Lothian	(B)
Social work area team – Strathclyde	(C)
Social work area team – Strathclyde	(D)
Specialist social work team – Strathclyde	(E)
Specialist voluntary organisation – Lothian	(F)
Specialist social work team – Strathclyde	(G)
District council housing office – Strathclyde	(H)
Specialist social work team – Lothian	(I)

The Perth and Kinross District Study (1991) presented the same four vignettes to workers in three social work teams, these being: a rural generic team; an adolescent unit; and a duty team in Perth. In total, 13 interviews were held for each vignette.

The people selected for interview

In each of the nine agencies we selected approximately eight workers for interview. Those interviewed were representative of workers involved in the assessment and/or management of clients. We were directed in this selection process by project leaders who identified workers with case loads or experience of working with clients who were or had been homeless. Where access to a key worker was governed by a receptionist, as in five case study locations, the vignettes were presented to the receptionists for assessment. In all cases the receptionist's role only extended as far as making an appointment for the potential client. No evidence of a screening process was observed. These interviews were not included in the agency's sample of interviews for analysis.

Categories of information

Data were collected from a series of open-ended questions exploring the inter-related themes of assessment, type and duration of intervention, and referrals. This section will outline these categories and point to various practice dilemmas which might be encountered.

(a) Assessment

The first kind of information drawn from the vignette analysis focuses on the assessment of potential clients.

Assessment is regarded as a key social work function. The task of assessment requires the worker to evaluate both the applicant's needs and wants (which do not necessarily coincide) and to assess whether the agency has a statutory obligation or measure of responsibility towards the applicant. Assessment becomes the grounding upon which the worker defines what response can be made to the young person's petition and the direction it might follow.

Ideally, assessment is considered to be part of an ongoing process. Through regular assessment the worker attempts to develop a relationship with the client, the success of which is argued to be crucial to both defining and undertaking effective action.

Whilst the desire for more information about the vignettes was often expressed, the vast majority of respondents stated that the "bare bones" of these cases were extremely familiar. During emergency presentations the worker usually has limited information to work with when deciding what to do, yet the immediate response to a potential client is crucial as it can determine whether future intervention will take place. Clients can be easily "lost to the system" if they do not perceive the agency's response to be adequate.

(b) Intervention types and duration

Each interviewee was asked to evaluate whether there was a role for the agency in responding to the young person's petition. They were asked to decide whether or not from their own experiences the young person would be taken up as a "case" or offered a range of short-term assistance and advocacy. Interviewees were then asked to catalogue the type of intervention they would offer the young person, and the constraints which would restrict this practice. Interviewees were also asked to define what outcomes they would consider to be the result of successful intervention and the likelihood of that being achieved.

If the interviewee could perceive no role for their agency they were asked to identify whether they would refer the young person to another agency and if they would support such a referral. Here the extent of inter-agency collaboration and the ability of the worker to gain access to other agencies becomes a key issue.

Findings

We present our findings case by case.

Vignette 1

Kenny

Kenny is 17. He was previously "on supervision" when he was 16, but this was discontinued when he was not responding to social work intervention. He has a known history of committing petty offences. His mother and father are separated and he has moved between their homes on a regular basis. He claims that each parent has now rejected him because he has a drink problem and has spent two nights on a friend's floor before being asked to leave. This is the third time he has presented as homeless in the last six months.

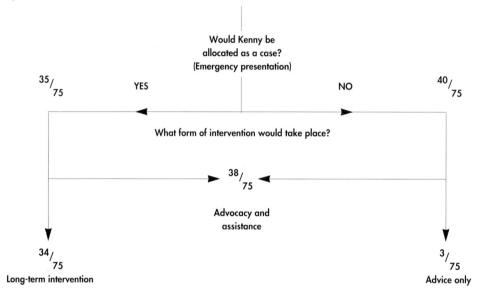

(a) Assessment

Kenny was identified as being characteristic of many young men who present themselves as homeless. Concern focused upon his petty offending, drinking behaviour and homeless situation. The possible inter-relatedness of these characteristics was also noted. Kenny was seen as "crying out for help", yet the task of defining an agency response to Kenny proved difficult.

Thirty-five interviewees believed that Kenny would be taken on as a case whilst 40 judged casework to be an unlikely outcome based on the information available. Workers in specialist housing and social work agencies tended to be clearer in either identifying or rejecting Kenny as a case, defining him as appropriate (E – a specialist team) or inappropriate (F,G,H – specialist and housing teams) for their programme. Workers in social work area teams (A,B,C,D) and one specialist social work team (I), did not present a uniform response to Kenny's application for assistance. This finding highlights an important dilemma faced by many social workers.

Some of the social workers interviewed noted that Kenny had previously been "on supervision" and this placed a moral responsibility upon the social work department to respond.

Others observed that he had presented three times previously, and had had an unsuccessful relationship with the social work department. This was felt to be characteristic of many young people coming into contact with social workers and would inhibit intervention. These latter were more likely to suggest that Kenny would want money and accommodation only, resources that the social work department cannot provide. Kenny would "probably walk out of the door" when this became apparent.

(b) Intervention

(i) **Emergency action and referrals.**
Only one of the agencies included in this study provided emergency accommodation (specialist team G). Seventy-two interviewees – i.e. nearly all of them – stated that with Kenny's approval they would attempt to help him find a bed for the night in an emergency hostel.

(ii) **Advocacy and assistance in the short-term**
Supported accommodation was seen as an essential component to helping Kenny in the longer term. With Kenny's consent efforts would be made to find "suitable" supported accommodation, for a medium to long term period. The term "suitable" here refers to finding accommodation which Kenny will find acceptable and will help him to progress towards independent living. Ideally, the support services would also address his needs with regard to alcohol abuse and offending. Whilst most referrals focused on supported accommodation, additional referrals would be made to alcohol advice centres and the housing department.

The specialist teams (E,F,G,H,I) included in the study would contact the social work department in order to attain a fuller assessment, especially of Kenny's self-professed drink problem and offending behaviour.

Approximately half of those interviewed wished to pursue the option of an attempted reconciliation of Kenny with his parents. These workers tended to stress the difficulties that Kenny would face if he remained homeless.

Two thirds of those interviewed would attempt to help Kenny run a benefit check. Here interviewees would act as "liaison" workers between Kenny and the DSS.

(iii) **Case work**
Of those who suggested that Kenny might well be allocated as a case, 34 thought they would be able to progress to long term case work. The progression to this type of intervention was seen to be dependent upon developing a good working relationship with Kenny, and finding stable supported accommodation which Kenny was prepared to maintain. Work here would concentrate on Kenny's offending and drinking behaviour.

(c) The definition of success

In most instances, finding Kenny 'stable' accommodation which he was able to maintain was viewed as a successful outcome to aim for.

(d) Constraints

The major concern all workers held was the assumed difficulty in making a successful referral to supported accommodation on Kenny's behalf. Interviewees believed that in the present housing environment, where very few vacancies exist, agencies can "pick and choose" whom they work with, and consequently it would be difficult to find Kenny a place.

Workers felt that much depended upon Kenny's attitude and motivation. Kenny, who like many young people, had probably not learnt the art of compromise and negotiation. Such youngsters are regarded as troublesome and difficult to work with.

In addition, it was thought that Kenny's drink problem would prohibit his access to much of the supported accommodation that is available. Indeed one agency (F – a specialist voluntary team) suggested that they would be unable to work with Kenny because of his drink problem. Finally, the low priority placed upon people experiencing difficulties similar to Kenny's by the social work department was perceived as a potential barrier to engaging with him.

(e) <u>The chances of a successful intervention</u>

The chances of success depend upon the constraints detailed above. With these in mind the majority felt that Kenny's chances were at best 50/50.

In the **Perth and Kinross District case study**, 11 of 13 workers believed that as social workers they held no statutory obligation towards Kenny. As a result Kenny would not be allocated as a case. Two workers thought that Kenny would at least become a short term case, identifying his vulnerability because of his age as the major factor in this decision. All 13 workers would engage with Kenny in an advisory capacity and attempt to help him find some accommodation. The major constraints to undertaking this work were seen as Kenny's co-operation and the lack of accommodation available, especially in the rural area. Workers did not hold out much hope of successfully addressing Kenny's drinking behaviour.

Vignette 2

Sheena

Sheena is 15 and has a daughter who is 5 months old. She is living with her mother, is doing well at school and wishes to continue. Whilst she is at school her mother looks after the child. The father of the child is in jail but will shortly be released, and Sheena intends to maintain contact with him. Her mother has told her that she will be thrown out of the house if she sees him again. Sheena now wants her own flat and says that she will petition herself as homeless when she is 16.

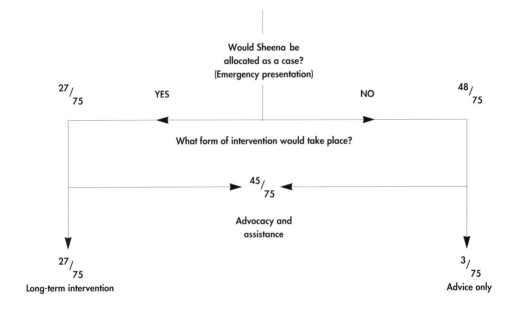

(a) Assessment

Concern focused around Sheena's own vulnerability because of her age, but predominantly upon the quality of care that her baby is receiving. Whilst it was noted that many women of Sheena's age are extremely competent and at present "things seem to be O.K.", a cautionary note was raised with regard to the changes which might arise when the father of the child leaves prison.

Twenty-seven out of the 75 workers interviewed believed that Sheena would be allocated as a case within their agency. Of the remaining 48 respondents, 45 suggested a short-term advocacy and assistance role would be more appropriate. Only 3 workers felt that an advice-only role would be their agencies' most appropriate response.

Workers in the four social work area teams (A,B,C,D) were equally undecided as to whether Sheena would become a case or not. Those social workers who believed that Sheena would not become a case chose to engage in a short-term monitoring role. Specialist agencies (E, F and G) were equally split; however, two specialist teams (Agencies I and H) felt that Sheena would be incorporated into their programmes.

(b) Intervention

(i) Emergency action and referrals

Emergency action is seen as less of a necessity in Sheena's case, a factor that would be to her advantage. Workers were concerned, however, to place Sheena in touch with housing professionals and would make referrals to housing advice centres, the homeless persons' officer and the district council.

(ii) Advocacy and assistance in the short-term

In the short term most workers sought to engage in a 'realistic' planning process, based on Sheena's consent. Typically, this would involve two components:

A. Exploring Sheena's ability to manage independently and especially her capacity to provide appropriate care arrangements for her baby. This work would be undertaken on the assumption that either Sheena will want to set up her own home in the near future or her present situation could be threatened.

This would involve guiding Sheena through the DSS benefit maze, introducing Sheena to support networks for single parents, and identifying supported accommodation suitable for a young mother. Workers not in an area team felt that a referral to an area team would be necessary to utilise social workers' "powers" as advocates to gain the best possible services for Sheena.

B. The second component would involve working with Sheena and her mother. At present Sheena's mother is seen as a key to helping Sheena manage with her infant and at school. Here the unknown history of the father of the child comes into question. If the father is in jail for reasons of petty offending workers would attempt to negotiate a solution to this impasse between Sheena and her mother. If the father is in jail for a more serious offence (such as a sexual offence) this would radically change the situation, but more information would be needed before an intervention path would be defined.

Specialist agency (G) felt that, initially, separate negotiations with Sheena and her mother would be the most appropriate course of action to follow.

Finally, some workers would examine the opportunities of gaining access to day care centres for Sheena's baby, to enable Sheena to continue her education.

(iii) Case work

Case work would include all the components above, including managing the input made by all other agencies and is envisaged as being for the longer term. Twenty-seven respondents stated that counselling, advocacy and support services would be provided until Sheena could manage independently in her own tenancy. The uncertainties which would influence the direction of case work depend on whether Sheena decides to remain with her mother or set up on her own, and on what happens when the father of her child returns. Here continued assessment through time is the key role identified by those interviewed.

(c) Defining success

On the whole success was defined as the creation or maintenance (if Sheena remains with her mother) of a safe, settled environment in which Sheena was able to look after her child.

(d) <u>Constraints</u>

Once again the client's agreement was seen as the first major barrier to overcome, although less so than with Kenny. The remaining constraints relate to a shortage of supported accommodation for single parents and the shortage of nursery places. It was felt that Sheena is unlikely to take her education very far.

(e) <u>The chances of a successful outcome</u>

Many felt Sheena's chances were good as she did not appear to be presenting in an emergency situation. Social workers 'like' people similar to Sheena as compared to Kenny. If Sheena's chances were qualified in any way that was because of uncertainties about Sheena's boyfriend, the father of the child.

In the **Perth and Kinross District case study**, all 13 workers expressed concern about care issues associated with Sheena's child. However, this did not guarantee Sheena's allocation as a case. Most workers perceived that teams were "bogged down with statutory work", and thus identified a monitoring role for themselves, dependent upon what happened when Sheena was 16 and gaining more information about the boyfriend. Sheena was evaluated as seeming to be secure at the moment, but workers felt that they would support any housing application she might make. If Sheena was allocated as a case in the adolescent unit, workers would at least attempt a reconciliation between Sheena and her mother, and if this was unsuccessful would help her move into her own home. Eleven workers would offer Sheena advice about benefits and housing, and six workers would discuss her future schooling.

The major constraint facing Sheena if she was in a rural area would be the lack of accommodation. On the whole, however, workers felt that Sheena would be regarded as a high priority by both housing and the DSS so her chances could be considered as good. No-one here, or in the centres contributing to our main study, thought of consulting staff doing probation or prison social work, although such people might know a good deal about the boyfriend.

Vignette 3

Robert

Robert came to the office and asked to see a social worker. He claimed that he was sleeping rough, and his appearance would appear to corroborate this. During this discussion Robert's attention drifted quite markedly and he seemed disinterested in the questions put to him. He looked to be around 16 or 17 years of age but did not disclose his date of birth.

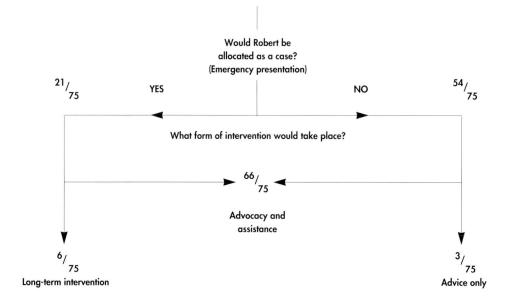

(a) Assessment

Several themes appeared in the preliminary assessment of Robert. First, concern was focused upon his apparently disinterested behaviour. Workers associated this with numerous possibilities, these being:

(a) Robert might be taking drugs or alcohol;

(b) Robert might be experiencing the effects of sleeping rough;

(c) Robert might have a mental health problem;

(d) Robert might be under 16 and attempting to protect his identity;

(e) Robert, like young people in general, may be distrustful of social workers; and/or,

(f) Robert, like many young people, might just be interested in getting some money.

Second, unless a mental health problem could be clearly defined, workers would on the whole attempt to deal with Robert according to the information he was prepared to disclose. One worker stated that she would,

> *"assume Robert was not wanting to be chased, so would have to go easy. You cannot force him to talk."*

Another suggested that,

> *"if he will only talk about money, then as a social worker there would be little I could offer him."*

Nevertheless, most workers would "attempt" to discover why Robert's attention was drifting.

Only 21 out of 75 workers interviewed felt that Robert would be allocated as a case. Many workers chose to leave the future allocation of Robert as a case "open", depending upon future assessments. Only six held out hope that long term intervention would be possible, and 66 believed that short term advocacy and assistance would be the likely focus of intervention. Social work area teams (B,C,D) and one of the specialist agencies (F) were most divided about whether to classify Robert as a potential case or not.

(b) Intervention

(i) Emergency action and referrals
Emergency action consisted of 'phoning round the various housing agencies and homeless units, in order to find Robert a bed for the night. In Glasgow, the Hamish Allan Centre and Stopover were frequently cited. In Edinburgh, Stopover was also cited but the demand for places was seen as so great that *any* hostel would be approached. If this proved impossible workers would advise Robert of places where he could get food and have a wash. Many of those social workers interviewed considered a possible cash payment to Robert, so that "at least he could buy some food". Only 3 workers would just advise Robert of the various hostels he could approach. All the specialist agencies would refer Robert to a social work area team for a fuller assessment.

(ii) Advocacy and assistance in the short-term
Provided that Robert returned for a further appointment, workers would begin to undertake a more thorough assessment of him. Here, work would be undertaken to find Robert a place in "appropriately" supported accommodation to match his needs, and importantly, his wants.

(iii) Case work
Only if a mental health, drugs or physical health problem could be discerned, or Robert proved to be under 16, would workers in area teams consider longer term case work. Under these circumstances they would have a statutory obligation to act. Interviewees not prepared to contemplate longer term case work felt that some other social work agency should help him.

(c) The definition of success

Success is seen as finding Robert a bed for the night and then meeting him for a further assessment. Finding longer term accommodation with appropriate support which Robert could maintain represents the extent of workers' hopes.

(d) Constraints

Overwhelmingly Robert's co-operation and the lack of availability of suitable accommodation, i.e., that which might match any of his presenting needs, were identified as the major barriers to effective intervention on Robert's behalf. Finding a stable environment for Robert was seen as crucial if any attempt was to be made to address his potential mental health, or drug related problems. In Lothian Region, it was felt that very few emergency hostel places existed, and the places that do exist are not suitable for a vulnerable young person. As for longer term accommodation places, which require planned admission, "few are available for someone like Robert".

(e) The chances of a successful intervention

The chances of providing or facilitating a successful solution to Robert's problems depend not only on scarce resources, but also on getting Robert to talk more openly. Robert might be the most vulnerable of all the vignettes presented, yet interviewees believed that he is the most likely *not* to receive a service. Robert would be unlikely to progress to the stage where social workers could use their specialist counselling and case management skills.

In the **Perth and Kinross District case study** only 1 worker out of 13 believed that Robert would become a case. Robert's unwillingness to provide more information impeded any decision on allocation. All workers were, however, prepared to assume some role. This varied between encouraging Robert to come back when he was willing to talk and providing a list of bed-and-breakfast accommodation. Despite concerns being raised about Robert's potential drink or drug abuse problem, as manifest in his drifting attention, under present circumstances there would be little scope for intervention. Success was seen as getting Robert to talk, providing a list of bed and breakfasts, and possibly finding out where his family is.

It seems clear that, with present powers and resources, little can be done for a youngster who may have serious mental health problems unless his behaviour becomes sufficiently dangerous or bizarre to compel attention – probably from mental hospitals or prisons.

Vignette 4

Kylie

Kylie is 17 and has recently been offered a flat under the homeless persons' legislation (one offer only). The flat has no furniture and she is unable to acquire such items through hire purchase. She is on a Youth Training Scheme, and so she does not qualify for income support (and hence Social Fund payments). She feels she would give up the flat if she could not get any furniture.

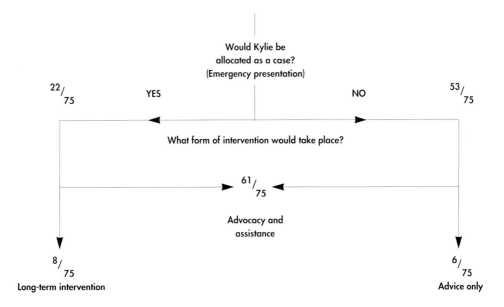

(a) Assessment

Concern focused on the danger of Kylie becoming roofless if she failed to find furniture for her flat. It was recognised that young people who have not been able to gather sufficient resources to furnish a flat find themselves in a position where they are *de facto* homeless, in that they cannot "live" in the flat. These young people are likely to give up the flat and become roofless, running the risk of being classified as "intentionally" homeless.

Twenty-two out of the 75 interviewed suggested that their agencies' ideal response would be to allocate Kylie as a case. However, only 8 identified case work as a likely outcome. The vast majority (61) of those interviewed, identified a short-term advocacy and assistance role as the more likely outcome. Kylie was seen as an extremely common kind of youngster, yet probably the least likely of all four vignettes to receive any *social work* help.

All workers (5) in housing agency (H), felt that they could place Kylie in a scatter flat and support her through case work for a minimum of six months. Three social workers (of 10) in social work area team (D) which collaborates with agency (H – housing) also hoped to place Kylie in such a scatter flat.

(b) Intervention

(i)   **Emergency action and referrals**
Other than a benefit check, those interviewed thought that there was little scope for emergency intervention in Kylie's case. Furthermore, unless an individual worker was aware of any furniture or household equipment that had been donated to their agency (a rare event) then workers would refer Kylie to those agencies which either sell second-hand furniture or attempt to help young people find such items.

(ii)   **Advocacy and assistance in the short-term**
Besides the above interventions social workers would attempt to help Kylie get a DSS "Crisis Loan", and consider a referral to an agency which provides furnished accommodation (such as agency H). Some would help Kylie write to charities.

(iii) **Case work**
Agency (H) would offer Kylie a place (dependent upon availability) in their supported and furnished accommodation, and specialist agency (I) might "at a later date", attempt to do the same and provide a negotiated amount of support.

(c) The definition of success

Success is quite simply defined as getting Kylie some furniture, or failing this, a move to a furnished tenancy.

(d) Constraints

Kylie does not hold a priority status with any of the agencies contacted and has few alternatives. She is considered to be in great danger of becoming roofless.

(e) The chances of a successful intervention

At the moment the chances of getting Kylie some furniture are seen as slim. Facilitating a move to furnished accommodation is also seen as difficult with few places being available. The chances of helping Kylie are, as one worker said "pretty remote at the moment".

In the **Perth and Kinross District case study**, *none* of those interviewed thought that Kylie would be allocated as a case. Workers in each agency felt that as she was over 16, on her own, had an income of sorts, and only wanted furniture, there was little their own agencies could do. Twelve workers defined success as Kylie finding some furniture. One worker would look for a loophole in the DSS regulations.

Conclusions

Employing the research technique of vignette data analysis, this Chapter has explored the nature of agency responses to young homeless people who present in crisis situations. In particular, valuable insights have been gained into the complex nature of "assessment", and the type of services offered to those young people who are not likely to be allocated as cases. Several conclusions can be drawn from this component of the research programme.

All four vignettes were interpreted as holding characteristics typical of many young people who present as homeless, and each vignette highlighted some of the difficulties encountered by workers attempting to help them.

Kenny, for example, had a one in two chance of being allocated as a case depending upon which agency and which worker he made contact with. Specialist agencies made a uniform response to Kenny, calculating whether his needs and demands matched their service or not. Social workers in area teams, however, were unable to make such clear cut distinctions. Some social workers stated that they held a "moral" responsibility to respond to Kenny because of his previous social work contact. Others pointed to a series of constraints which they felt were likely to inhibit intervention.

Kenny was thought to be typical of young people, who are regarded as not being able to negotiate, disruptive, and holding a fixed set of *wants* which do not necessarily match their *needs*. Social workers predicted that a successful intervention would depend upon his attitude. Furthermore, social workers recognise that people like Kenny have a low social work priority, and scarce social work resources have more pressing demands made upon them. Finally, social workers observed that the housing environment provides limited opportunities, especially with regard to supported accommodation. They believed they would find it extremely difficult and time consuming to find Kenny a safe and secure housing environment.

The impact of these constraints is that social workers are likely to set a limited range of work objectives and believe that the probability of achieving them are a matter of chance. Under these circumstances, Kenny would "probably" walk out the door!

Robert held a one in three chance of being allocated as a case. However, nearly all of those interviewed would engage in a short-term advocacy and assistance role. Robert was seen as likely to experience similar resourcing problems to Kenny unless a range of factors became evident which might lead to him being allocated as a priority case. Robert was seen as *potentially* the most vulnerable of all the vignettes, yet unless he was more open he would be almost certain to remain homeless.

Sheena also held a one in three chance of being allocated as a case, yet was more likely to receive *successful* intervention, because she has not presented in a crisis situation. This affords workers time to engage in a more "realistic" planning process. The main reason workers would engage with Sheena, however, focuses around their statutory child care obligations. In other words, Sheena would receive assistance primarily because of her baby. If her present environment broke down, however, workers were concerned that supported accommodation, especially for single parents, is extremely limited. This situation is more chronic in rural areas as highlighted by the Perth and Kinross case study.

Kylie, however, is seen as the least likely to be successfully helped outside a specialist agency. She holds a low priority, and would not receive the resources required to meet her needs. She is in great danger of becoming roofless.

The four vignettes all contribute to our understanding of the dilemmas faced by social workers when dealing with young people. As one interviewee stated,

"We are dealing with a growing number of young people (over 16 years old) who we find difficult to define in terms of a response. We are faced with problems as to what cut-off age we should deal with and what categories of vulnerability we should consider. As social workers, we find it difficult to say no, but just who should you prioritise? We need to be stricter with ourselves, otherwise the situation could get out of control."

Two clear dilemmas emerge from this research. First, social workers have to decide whether they ought to respond to a young person's demands. Second, if a response is to be made, they have to consider how they can provide a fast and effective service. In social work area teams these dilemmas appear to result in an uncertain and rather arbitrary decision making process. This cannot be helpful to the young person or the worker concerned. The uncertainty is derived from the complexity of the interpretative work which has to be undertaken, and the severe time and resource constraints under which social workers have to act.

There is a clear need here to involve specialists in developing a "standardised" assessment model, to be made easily understandable to the young person. This should have the purpose of enabling social workers to make clear distinctions as to what action can, and should, be undertaken in emergency situations, and for different client groups amongst the young homeless population. This process would enable the worker to broadly classify needs, take a care package "off the shelf", or identify which agency would be best suited to addressing the young person's demands.

It is clear, however, that little progress can be made in these directions unless the resources of: (1) housing; (2) cash benefits from social security or other sources, and (3) trained social and support workers become more plentiful. Those three developments need to be combined and coordinated, and that will not happen unless policy decisions are taken at central and local levels of government to make an effective response to the needs of young people like these. Those decisions would have to be implemented by clearly incorporating responsibilities to provide services for these youngsters in community care plans and housing plans. The effects of the changes made in 1988 in the social security benefits for young people must also be frankly re-appraised and new provisions made.

We return to these issues in our concluding Chapters.

Chapter 5

Social Work With Homeless Young People: Monitoring Live Cases

Introduction

Having described the response of agencies to standardised but imaginary examples, we examine the work actually done for those young people whom these agencies accept as "cases". In each of the nine study settings an average of nine "live" cases were monitored over a 3 month period. The overall aim of this part of the study was to gain insight into the nature of social work with young homeless people. Focusing on the cases they currently held, social workers were asked about the original referral, what they had done and were attempting to do and how optimistic they were about the outcome.

Of the 80 "live" cases monitored, there were an equal number of male and female clients. The majority were aged between 16 and 18, although cases were drawn also from the 19 to 25 year old age group. Most became cases as a result of experiencing difficulties associated with: offending; abuse (physical, sexual or emotional); mental health; concern about the care of their own children; or drug abuse.

This Chapter begins with a detailed account of two cases which exemplify many of the features of the 80 cases on which data were collected. These cases are followed by a more general discussion of social work with the young homeless, in which a fundamental distinction is made between area team and specialist team practice. The distinction is further illustrated by a number of selected case studies. The Chapter ends with a listing of good practice in work with the young homeless.

Two cases

The "interviews" referred to in these two cases are those which we conducted with the social workers.

> **Kenneth:** is sixteen and a half years old and was referred to area team (A) when his father and step-mother defined him as outwith parental control. Since initial referral to social work, Kenneth has had 18 different case placements and he has absconded from all of them. In the month previous to the first interview with his social worker she had found him a place in an adolescent unit. This started well but Kenneth struck a member of staff and left. Since then he has been roofless.
>
> At the first interview the social worker reported that she had succeeded in obtaining a district council tenancy. Kenneth accepted it but failed to keep the necessary appointments to ensure that the utilities were connected. She had just arranged another appointment. Over the next month she intends to help Kenneth apply for a community care grant to furnish his flat and she will also apply for a section 24 grant as a 'back-up'.
>
> At the second interview the social worker reported that Kenneth had failed to keep several further appointments to have his utilities connected. She had

also heard from the Social Fund officer that Kenneth did not qualify. Moreover, since he had failed to sign on, he was no longer eligible to receive social security payments. Kenneth's father had been enlisted to persuade him to keep a further appointment to have his utilities connected, but also without success. Kenneth had continued to see his social worker and she had re-applied for the district council flat. A section 24 grant had been secured to buy furniture, but as she had not had time to administer it, she had lodged it with a voluntary organisation "Follow-up".

Over the next month the social worker intends to enquire why Kenneth's application for a community care grant was refused. She would also like to re-allocate the case because she feels she has not sufficient time to devote to his needs.

At the third interview in November Kenneth's case was still held by the same social worker but she was extremely frustrated. Having been refused control of the money held by 'Follow-up', Kenneth had alternated between sleeping rough and lodging with part of his extended family. He had again failed to sign-on, and as a consequence, his benefits had been stopped. The social worker feels that Kenneth cannot manage independently and needs supported accommodation. He has refused all offers and generally seems incapable of planning his future.

Deirdre: is eighteen and a half years old and was referred to specialist voluntary agency (F) after being sexually abused by her step-father and subsequently absconding from her care placement.

Following initial referral 2 years ago, the social worker had built a good relationship with Deirdre and had helped her come to terms with her earlier experience of rape and prostitution. Deirdre had also been helped to control the aggressive behaviour which had led to her being asked to leave her flat. She had recently been allocated a new place in one of the agency's other residential units.

At the time of the first interview Deirdre had just become pregnant. On learning about her condition, her mother re-established contact and claimed she wanted to help her. The social worker had helped Deirdre come to terms with her boyfriend and the new situation with her mother. The residential support worker had helped her develop practical living skills. According to this support worker, Deirdre regarded shopping as appropriate only for old people and was completely incapable of budgeting.

At the second interview the social worker reported that while she had been successful in helping Deirdre come to terms with her boyfriend, she had not managed to effect a reconciliation with her mother. The 'sticking point' was that her mother still wanted her to write a letter to her step-father stating that he had not abused her. Deirdre was unprepared to do this. As far as accommodation was concerned, Deirdre had turned down the offer of a single parent flat on the grounds that her boyfriend couldn't join her, but the support worker had succeeded in getting her a housing association flat. She also felt she was making progress with Deirdre's budgeting and shopping skills.

> At the third interview, it was reported that Deirdre continued to have nothing to do with her mother but that she and her boyfriend seemed to have a good relationship. However, the offer of the housing association flat had fallen through, and since the support worker had been on holiday, the social worker had applied for a district council flat. This had just been allocated and the social worker was going to arrange the move and apply for a community care grant for furnishings.

The Kenneth and Deirdre cases illustrate a number of recurrent features of young homeless people and social work with them.

First, in relation to their family backgrounds, both Deirdre and Kenneth experienced the effects of their parents' divorce and remarriage. In both cases there is also the suggestion of abuse. While such experiences are not universal they were depressingly common in the 80 cases followed over the 3 month periods.

Second, in relation to previous social work contact, the 3 month monitoring period represented only an episode in both Deirdre and Kenneth's long-term contact with social workers. In all 80 cases studied, only a handful had had no previous contact with social work.

Third, in relation to events over the 3 month period, both cases illustrate the highly volatile nature of these young people's lives. Kenneth alternated between living in an adolescent unit, sleeping rough and lodging with extended family members. Over the same 3 month period Deirdre became pregnant, planned to move into one flat and was just about to move into another. The majority of case studies reveal similar and even greater volatility over the observation period: e.g. Charles stayed with his mother (twice) had a place in a supported hostel and spent a short period in jail; Simon disappeared halfway through the period, and is presumed to be in London. These examples could be multiplied many times over but they provide eloquent testimony of the volatile and dislocated nature of the lives of these young people.

Fourth, in relation to client behaviour, Kenneth (but Deirdre to a lesser extent) illustrates the unreliability of most young homeless people as social work clients. Despite having numerous appointments made for him, Kenneth repeatedly failed to turn up. He also changed his mind about the kind of accommodation he wanted. The transcripts of most other cases are replete with missed appointments, failures to carry out agreed courses of action and inexplicable changes of mind. There are, of course, many reasons why young homeless people make "difficult" social work clients owing to their previous experiences of abuse and disappointment, poor communication and coping skills and volatile life styles.

Fifth, in relation to the scope of social work intervention, both cases reveal the need to go beyond the young person as client. In the 3 month observation period Kenneth's social worker had to contact and negotiate with the district council housing department, two DSS officers, Kenneth's father and an agency offering supported accommodation. Over the same period Deirdre's social worker had to work with a residential support worker, Deirdre's mother, her boyfriend, a housing association, the district council housing department and the DSS office. This catalogue of contacts is not unusual: in the transcripts of the 80 cases there are references to all of the above, but also to the police, reporters to the children's panel, landlords, fellow tenants, alcoholism counsellors, GPs, psychiatrists, drug workers and local councillors.

Having identified these common features in the Deirdre and Kenneth cases, a number of differences are also apparent.

There can be no doubt that Kenneth is the more "difficult" of the two cases. Only sixteen and a half years old, he has already absconded from 18 different care placements. His lifestyle is more dislocated and he is more unreliable as a client. His homelessness "career" is further developed. It is perhaps not accidental that he also experiences a different kind of social work intervention. His social worker is exclusively concerned with securing him accommodation and benefits, and, by her own admission, has not sufficient time to devote to his other needs. Deirdre, by comparison, enjoys a confiding relationship with her social worker who has helped her come to terms with her past and to sort out her relationship to her mother and boyfriend. The residential support worker has also given her practical instruction in "life skills".

It is suggested that these differences are not accidental but reflect a fundamental distinction between the kind of support provided by generic area team workers and that provided by specialist workers in specialist teams. Kenneth represents the kind of client typically seen by the area teams and his experiences over the three month period exemplify the kind of social work in most area teams. While Deirdre may not be the typical client seen by the specialist teams (they are extremely varied) the kind of support she received over the three month period is more common in the specialist team.

Evidence for this suggestion may be found throughout the 80 completed case studies, but for present purposes 10 will suffice. Five case studies will be presented to illustrate common features in the management of cases in social work area teams; they will be followed by five case studies to illustrate common features in case management in specialist teams.

Case management in Social Work Area Teams

The "interviews" referred to in the accounts which follow are those we conducted with the workers concerned.

> **Case 1: Martin, 16 years old, referred to social work area team (C) following periods in care and sleeping rough.**
> At the first interview with his social worker it was explained that Martin needed a home away from his step family on the grounds that he was "an escapee from a multi-problem extended family who has had violence perpetrated on him for years". As yet the social worker has not approached the district council housing department, partly because Martin wants to get right away from the area, and partly because of the pressing demands of child protection work. Over the next month she said that she would attempt to get him a permanent tenancy, but she was not hopeful since the housing department did not place a high priority on youth homelessness and had not developed any special initiatives.
> At the second interview no further progress had been made on the case. Martin was trying to find work and the social worker was going to try and get him a tenancy in the adjoining rural district where he has been staying with his girlfriend's family.
> At the third interview the social worker reported that Martin had found a job, but that she had failed to find a tenancy. The rural district housing office had followed-up Martin's application but had decided that he would be better housed in his own area. The local housing officer had been approached but he claimed to have no knowledge of Martin's case. Accordingly, the social worker now intended to re-apply to the rural district housing office

explaining Martin's need for a tenancy outwith his area and away from his family. She also intended to enlist Martin's councillor to support the application.

Case 2: Charles, 17 years old on probation with social work area team (A) following eviction from his mother's home and a string of offences, including glue sniffing and drunkenness.

At the first interview the social worker had just obtained Charles a tenancy in a district council furnished flat. She was concerned that Charles did not break this tenancy (as he had done with three previous tenancies). She intends to see him on a fortnightly basis until his probation term ends.

At the second interview the social worker reported that she had been successful in getting Charles a section 24 grant to enable him to purchase items not included in the furnished flat. She claimed to be pleased with his progress but was already concerned about what he will do when he becomes 18 and his benefit entitlements will change for the worse.

At the third interview Charles had successfully completed his community service and he had a YTS job. His girlfriend had moved in with him and he seemed to be "settling down". The social worker was about to go on maternity leave and was making arrangements to transfer the case. She was concerned that he would not be seen as a priority case when the anticipated crisis occurred following his 18th birthday.

Case 3: Harvey, 20 year old presented himself as homeless to social work area team (C) and was offered a guest house address and money for his bus fares.

At the interview 3 weeks after his initial presentation, Harvey had again presented as homeless, having been asked to leave the guest house for not paying his rent. The social worker telephoned the guest house but was unable to get an explanation of the circumstances surrounding his departure. He also 'phoned the DSS office to obtain a Crisis Loan but was informed that Harvey had only recently received such a loan – a fact which Harvey denied.

At the second interview the social worker reported that Harvey had called again to say that he had failed to find accommodation and that he now needed clothing as well. He had assisted Harvey complete an application for a Community Care Grant and had given him a letter to present to the WVS for clothing.

At the third interview the social worker reported that he had received a court request for a background report on Harvey, who had been remanded on a drunk and incapable charge. The report had been sent but the Sheriff had criticised it on the grounds that it contained no evidence of suitable post-release accommodation. The social worker had to acknowledge that he had failed, but emphasised that he was powerless. All he felt he was able to do was to telephone for hostel vacancies, but these only came up infrequently and were unlikely to be suitable for someone with an alcohol problem. He anticipates that on his release Harvey will again present to the intake team.

Case 4: Karen, 16 year old referred to area team (B) following a period in care and an unsuccessful attempt at reconciliation with her mother.

At the first interview with her social worker it was reported that Karen had recently been given a tenancy in a district council flat and a section 24 grant. The requirement of both was that she maintained regular contact with her social worker. She hadn't, and had presented herself to the intake team with a budgeting crisis. The social worker had offered her advice and guidance.

At the second interview the social worker reported that Karen had not kept an appointment for a job interview and she had agreed to accompany her for any future interviews. Moreover, he was able to report that Karen had been searching second hand shops for furniture and that she had successfully fended-off friends from staying in her flat (and putting the tenancy in jeopardy). Budgeting remained a problem and the social worker had decided to keep some social work funds "in account for her".

At the third interview the social worker reported that Karen's sister had moved in with her and that it seemed to be a stable arrangement. Karen had also succeeded in meeting an appointment with her career officer to discuss yet another YTS place, and she had been able to budget for her first fuel bill. The social worker was reasonably optimistic but intended to keep her case open while the section 24 money lasted.

Case 5: Duncan, 17 years old. Estranged from his family and recently returned from London to be seen by intake worker in social work area team (A).

He has been allocated an unfurnished district council flat in a "bad" estate within the city. The duty worker has advised him of the hardship grants, Crisis Loans and Community Care Grants which might be available to him and has assisted him in completing a claim form. Duncan's file will remain closed, but if he is unsuccessful in his claim it is likely that he will return for further advice and assistance.

The nature of social work intervention in all five cases exhibits many of the characteristics already identified in the Kenneth case. It is reactive, almost exclusively concerned with accommodation and benefits; it affords few examples of planned case management and much of the work could equally well be done by a suitably staffed housing department.

This is particularly apparent in the two cases (Harvey and Duncan) dealt with by duty or intake workers. The common features of generic area team work will be explored further at a later stage, but for present purposes it is necessary to acknowledge that the cases also illustrate some variations in area team practice. The Martin and Harvey cases both come from an area team (C) which has a high turnover of staff, few of whom have knowledge of the local area. Moreover, it is acknowledged to have poor liaison arrangements with its district council housing department, which in turn attaches low priority to youth homelessness. The team members feel that they are only able to help a few young people and are rarely able to engage in case work. When it happens, as in the Martin case, it is rather ineffectual. [For many homeless young people presenting to this team the extent of social work intervention consists of being given section 12 money to enable them travel elsewhere (usually Glasgow) in search of accommodation.]

By any criteria the standard of practice in this team is poor. This is partly a result of the high turnover and limited experience of staff but it is also a direct consequence of the resource environment in which the team has to operate. The local housing department has no initiatives for the young homeless and it accords them low priority. Overall, area team (C) provides support for the contention that good social work practice requires good housing practice.

By contrast, the Charles and Karen cases both come from an area team (A) which has established good liaison arrangements with several local voluntary agencies which provide good quality accommodation and specialist skills. The team has also established an efficient advice system and has a clear referral procedure to the homeless person's officer at the district council housing department. These resources and arrangements are reflected in the management of the two cases. Over the 3 month observation period there is evidence that the social workers have been able to go beyond the provision of accommodation and benefits and they have helped Charles and Karen establish more settled lifestyles.

Effective collaboration with a good housing service is not an alternative to good social work; it makes good social work possible. And that, in turn helps the housing service.

Having discussed and illustrated the extremes of good practice in Area Teams A and C, it is worth summarising the achievements of Area Teams B and D.

Team B works with significant numbers of young homeless people, a result of its setting, and has built up a wealth of experience and contacts in this field. For those young people who are allocated as cases social workers offer significant amounts of support despite heavy case loads. Where feasible, the Team attempts to enable other agencies to manage young people in supported accommodation. The pattern of case management in team D is similar to that in other social work teams. Only extremely vulnerable people reach case status, and a combination of limited resources and the young person's immaturity prohibit effective management. The bulk of young people are assisted on a duty basis, contact is sporadic and workers usually have to react to crisis presentations.

Case management in specialist social work teams

We turn next to five cases dealt with by the specialist social work teams

> **Case 1: Arnold, 16 year old who self-referred to specialist social work team (G) after eviction from family home for violent and disruptive behaviour.**
>
> At the time of self-referral Arnold was sleeping in a coal shed. The team referred him to the local Homeless Persons Unit for accommodation and joint collaborative work was begun with the area team social worker (who held his probation order), the Homeless Persons Unit and a local ex-offender centre which offered a job scheme. Regular case conferences were held to obtain a comprehensive assessment and to review progress. A care assistant attached to the team was allocated to the case.
>
> At the second interview the social worker reported that Arnold was continuing with his work on YTS and CSO programmes but was experiencing difficulty with his landlord, who claimed that he was not keeping the rules. The care assistant has been allocated the task of helping Arnold to find alternative accommodation and his probation social worker has agreed to ask the Sheriff to adjust his reparation fine.
>
> At the third interview the care assistant reported that she and Arnold had visited a supported hostel run by a voluntary organisation. Arnold had appeared interested and a place had been applied for and allocated. Having

been in contact with his mother Arnold then made it clear that he wished to return to the family home. At the time of the third interview he had been back with his mother for a fortnight. During this time he had been arrested and had spent a weekend in jail. The incident was not serious and his mother offered bail and took him back home. Team members were currently helping Arnold and his mother to reconcile their earlier difficulties and plan for the future.

Case 2: Agnes, 17 year old referred to Specialist Team (E) by a social work area team.

Agnes was found temporary accommodation in a local stopover and an application was submitted for supported accommodation. Throughout her stay in the stopover temporary accommodation the team was undertaking a thorough assessment. Her mood swings and disruptive behaviour were monitored and regular case conferences were held between the specialist team and key workers from stopover.

At the second interview Agnes was still in her temporary accommodation and her behaviour towards other residents was often unacceptable, particularly following drinking bouts. Regular case conferences were continuing, but at the last one Agnes had refused to participate. It had become apparent that she was unhappy with her YTS placement and her social worker was going to try and find her more congenial work.

At the third interview the social worker reported that she had spent a good deal of time with Agnes over the last month and had persuaded her to undertake psychiatric counselling to help her deal with drinking and behaviour problems. She had also found her supported accommodation and Agnes had moved in. She will continue to visit her weekly and to hold monthly reviews.

Case 3: Stuart, 18 year old referred to specialist social work team (I) following his eviction from a district council tenancy.

Stuart had been offered accommodation in a shared flat with three other young people and a caretaker. His social worker had offered counselling for his immaturity. "Stuart is demonstratively gay and has not learned the art of compromise in his relations with his neighbours".

At the second interview the social worker reported that Stuart had not conformed to the flat rules, he had not paid his share of the fuel costs and had invited a boyfriend (and known drug user) to stay with him.

At the third interview the social worker reported that Stuart had been given an ultimatum. He had initially agreed to pay his bills and to eject his boyfriend. But he had not kept his earlier promise and has now been given 2 months' notice. The social worker will support an application for Stuart's own tenancy, providing he pays his outstanding debts. Stuart has accepted his condition and has obtained a full-time job to help pay off his debts. The case will remain open.

Case 4: Peter, 18 year old referred to a joint housing and social work project teams H and D following alternating periods of rooflessness and residential care.

Peter's support worker conducted an assessment and concluded that his major requirement was for intensive support. He obtained him a place in a supported scatter flat.

At the first interview, the support worker reported that Peter had taken up the tenancy on a trial basis. The contract specified that he would keep appointment with his support worker, homemaker and workers at a local drugs project. For the first week the support worker had visited Peter daily, but on finding him to be a good tenant, he had reduced the frequency of visits to twice per week. Meanwhile, Peter's homemaker (allocated by the social work department) had begun to help Peter cope at a practical level. She had instructed him in shopping, cooking, budgeting and healthy eating.

At the second interview Peter's support worker reported general satisfaction with his tenancy and his homemaker reported continued progress with his budgeting. Peter still has severe financial problems and she is concerned that he will resort to money lenders. She has negotiated more favourable repayment terms with public companies.

At the third interview the support worker reported continued satisfaction with his tenancy, apart from his experiment in mice breeding. He also reported that Peter had started a hairdressing course at a local college and appeared to be enjoying it. Given the evident progress it has been decided that the homemaker will be responsible for future monitoring, only involving the support worker when necessary.

Case 5: Mathew, 18 year old referred to specialist voluntary agency (E) following eviction from the family home.

Mathew had been involved in a serious motorbike accident in which a friend had died. His violent and erratic behaviour had increased following a hospital stay and he was not encouraged to return home. He had been in one of the agency's residential units for 10 months.

At the first interview his social worker explained that he was continuing to concentrate on Mathew's behavioural problems and a support worker was attempting to teach him essential life skills. Mathew had not been attending his YTS placement, despite help and encouragement from the support worker. She had found him a job but he had left it after only a fortnight.

At the second interview the support worker reported that Martin had remained unemployed for a fortnight but that he had then applied (successfully) for a hotel job. His shift work had prevented him from maintaining regular contact with his social worker. It had been decided that the support worker would continue as the regular link.

At the third interview the support worker reported that Mathew was still working at the hotel and appeared to be managing both his money and his time-keeping. She felt that the situation was stabilising, and if it continued for another month it would be appropriate to review his position in the project and assess whether an alternative form of support could be offered.

All of the above cases exhibit many of the characteristics already identified in the Deirdre case. Overall, the social work involvement is long term, it is sensitive to the needs of homeless young people (sometimes to the point of indulgence), it attempts to deal with the behavioural roots of their problems and it helps to prepare them for independent living.

The contrast between the management of these cases and those managed by the area teams is striking, but it has to be acknowledged it reflects differences in resources as well as differences in practice.

The workers in the social work area teams gave the impression of being continually "bombarded" with cases, those involving suspected abuse always having priority. As a consequence, opportunities for non-statutory case work are limited, and where they exist, there are time constraints on each case.

The workers in the specialist teams have more control over the volume of referrals and the types of clients they take on. They do not give the impression of being "bombarded". By comparison with their area team colleagues, they see their clients more regularly, and when they do see them, it is for longer periods. But it is what they do with and for them which deserves closer scrutiny.

Even with these extremely difficult clients there are attempts to undertake needs-led rather than service-led assessments. There are a number of instances, but the Agnes case provides the best example. Throughout her stay in temporary accommodation she was being assessed to help determine the most appropriate care "package". Such a lengthy assessment might be expected from a team which specialises in support to young people in temporary accommodation. Team members are experienced and give every impression of finding their work satisfying.

There is also evidence, in all cases, of a concerted attempt to monitor and review. In Arnold's case his support worker enlisted the help of the probation worker from the area team, a worker from the Homeless Persons' Unit and one from an Ex-offenders' Unit. Monitoring is also enhanced by the employment of and close collaboration with support workers, as illustrated in the cases involving Agnes, Peter and Arnold. Indeed, in Peter's case, responsibility for regular monitoring was devolved to the homemaker.

The major role of such support workers is, of course, to provide practical help and support on a more regular basis and for longer periods than trained social work staff can offer. Given that almost all of the cases studied exhibited various degrees of practical incompetence, such support workers play a vital role in prevention and rehabilitation.

One final feature of specialist teams' practice deserves highlighting; namely mediation and reconciliation between estranged parents and children. The Deirdre and Arnold cases provide evidence of such attempts and they deserve wider recognition. The social work team to which Arnold referred himself (G) specialises in work with teenagers and their families who are experiencing relationship difficulties at home. The project stresses the "normality of facing difficulties with such complicated relationships", and strives to facilitate their resolution and hence prevent the teenager becoming homeless. This includes the provision of respite accommodation and counselling. With those young people who cannot resolve their familial disputes, work is undertaken to help them work towards a position in which they can manage independently. This project deserves to be better known.

Other specialist teams

Features of the other specialist teams are worth summarising. Specialist Team F is a voluntary agency. Social workers act in tandem with residential support workers, the supporting worker making regular reports to the agency social worker. Strenuous efforts are also made to co-ordinate joint work between agency and area team staff. No time limit is set upon the resolution of cases because the agency recognises that individuals develop at different speeds and require a range of flexible support and counselling. While clients are required to leave the supported accommodation when mistakes are made, relationships are maintained, either to facilitate the move to alternative accommodation or to help re-integrate the client to the supported accommodation on a new contract. The Team is one of the few agencies which offers supported accommodation in the region, and it receives too many referrals, many of which are inappropriate. There is a clear need for a screening process and better liaison with referring agencies. It also has to be acknowledged that the agency has not developed clear policies for terminating and transferring cases. Workers carry cases for long periods and it is arguable that they might be more effective if they concentrated on shorter and more intensive interventions.

There are several examples of good practice undertaken by specialist Team (E). Intervention is focused on a young person's own needs and development pace and workers do not offer 'standardised' services.

Responsibilities for case management are shared between a qualified social worker, and a designated support worker. The social worker manages the case and advocates on behalf of the young person, the support worker has more regular contact and works on a range of practical issues. Young people tend not to regard this team as a social work team, and workers are not seen as social workers. As a result, they are more likely to strike up good working relationships with team members. Good practice is impeded by the fact that the team receive many inappropriate referrals from both the housing and the social work departments. Much time is wasted in attempting to make appropriate re-referrals. Young people often give up under these circumstances and are consequently "lost to the system". The setting is also a problem, the offices are located in an "unsafe" area which young people are reluctant to visit at night.

Finally, the joint Housing-Social Work Project (H and D) offers a unique service which grew out of a successful Urban Aid Project. Its unique features consist in the use of homemakers (to teach practical basic living skills), housing support workers (to provide counselling and long term support) and scatter flats (to avoid concentration in ghettos). The work of the agency provides one of the best examples of preventive and rehabilitative work in the young homeless field.

Conclusions

The monitoring of live cases reported in this Chapter has highlighted the different opportunities for social work practice in area and specialist teams. It is important to re-emphasise that these differences are rooted in the human resources each is able to devote to young homeless people, and in the priorities they have been given. In the area teams young homeless people compete for the social workers' time with all other client groups and it is not at all clear how much attention they should be given. In the specialist teams they do not compete and priorities are clearer. As a consequence, opportunities for assessment and care management are greater in the specialist teams and team managers have more experience of and confidence for this kind of work. Likewise, youngsters gain more confidence in them.

A similar argument for specialisation can probably be advanced for most client groups and there may be an overall move from generic to specialist practice over the next decade. In most instances this is likely to be a move to specialism *within* teams rather than between teams. However, even if such changes do occur, they cannot offer a complete solution. Specialisation is only possible in the larger centres where large case loads make that possible. Homelessness, however, arises everywhere. Many homeless youngsters come from families with a long history of contacts with the social work services, and it may be important to maintain continuity of care and build on the relationships established over many years. Homelessness may not be the fundamental problem: indeed it may be the result of child abuse, addiction, mental illness or other problems originating among other members of the family. With several services potentially in play, affecting several members of the household, it will be important to coordinate different kinds of work and decide priorities between them. Therefore, the immediate requirement is to raise the general standard of area team practice. Our recommendations, which will be developed in the last Chapter, call for various forms of "technology transfer" from those teams where good practice is common to those where it is rare. Examples of the kinds of good practice which the study revealed are listed below:

1 *Deployment of staff who are familiar with the lifestyles of young homeless people and able to "speak their language"*. When young homeless people described staff as "not like social workers" they were paying them a compliment.

2 *The use of time-limited goal setting designed to achieve specified things within a specified time*. Workers who operated in this fashion were less likely to feel despondent (even when failures occurred) than those who operated in an unstructured and open-ended fashion.

3 *Regular monitoring and review of cases*. Despite the chaotic lifestyles of their clients, workers in the most successful teams were able to review them at regular intervals, and, when appropriate, change their intervention strategy.

4 *Compilation and maintenance of up-to-date information on local resources*. Workers who had access to such information felt they were able to offer something; those who didn't felt powerless. In one of the busiest area teams an information desk has proved successful.

5 *Close liaison and regular meetings with staff from the local authority housing department*. The most effective arrangements involved contact at both managerial and basic worker levels.

6 *Clearly understood referral arrangements between social work and other agencies*. The best examples of such arrangements occurred between some social work teams and the Homeless Person's Officer in the housing department; the worst examples were between social work area teams and voluntary agencies.

7 *Use of support workers to supplement social work intervention*. They were invaluable in helping young homeless people to acquire basic life skills and in many cases were able to establish and maintain closer relationships than social workers.

8 *Use of allocation meetings and case conferences as learning opportunities for basic grade staff*. Basic grade staff need familiarisation before they have to deal with cases themselves. The practice of inviting them to allocation meetings provided them with such an opportunity.

9 *Social worker accompaniment for clients being interviewed by other agencies*. Workers in the most successful teams often accompanied clients. This practice was time-consuming but, given the vulnerability of many clients, it was probably cost-efficient.

10 *Promotion of mediation and reconciliation between young homeless people and their parents*. Most examples of good practice were concentrated in one team (G). They included contracts with family members to achieve casework goals, systematic reviews and the establishment of a step-parent group.

We showed our findings to many people with long experience in this field. This Chapter can be fittingly concluded with the summary offered by one of those who advised us.

"A number of points do clearly emerge – and they are ones which social work experience in general would endorse:

(i)   Work with young homeless people – especially those damaged through disrupted childhood experiences – is intractable and time-consuming;

(ii) A work context which is based on good inter-agency liaison, and acceptance of service responsibilities by other agencies such as housing providers, enhances the prospect of effective work;

(iii) Work which has access to sustained supportive services such as homemakers, is better placed to meet practical needs of young people and closely monitor their progress;

(iv) A work model – based *solely* on an "intake" approach of short term problem solving (e.g. welfare rights advocacy, housing allocation and short term home making) does not meet the needs of seriously damaged adolescents; and

(v)   It works against the prospects of stable sustained work when staff turnover is high. Staff lack experience, staff morale is low and other work priorities, especially child protection, consistently 'intrude' to the detriment of work with the young adult."

Chapter 6

The Scottish Survey Of Social Work And Housing Authorities

Introduction

As we began to reflect upon the conclusions to be drawn from the research reported in the last three Chapters we felt the need to consult the experts whose work we would be writing about. This Chapter reports the findings of a survey of social work and housing authorities in Scotland on aspects of youth homelessness. It provides a broad policy and practice backcloth upon which the case study component of the research programme can be located and draws on the experience of experts to test preliminary recommendations emerging from our research.

The survey was conducted on a cross-section of both urban and rural authorities. Recognising that the scale of homelessness is greater in urban settings, and that they are more likely to have developed innovative policy and practice, it was decided to contact all urban authorities and approximately half of the rural authorities.

The problem of social work and housing authorities not always sharing the same administrative boundaries was met by selecting social work target areas which provided the best match with district housing authority areas. The survey was carried out in December and January 1991/92. In total, 80 interview targets were identified, of which 75 were able to respond.

The findings

(I) Is there a problem?

The first issue explored by the survey was whether or not respondents perceived there to be a youth homelessness problem in their area. In total, 68 out of 75 respondents believed that housing amongst young people *was* a problem in their area. When the data are disaggregated, it is evident that both social work and housing managers are equally concerned about this problem.

Table One

Is housing amongst young people a problem in your area?

	Social Work	Housing	Aggregate
Yes	34	34	68
No	3	4	7

Valid cases 75:   Missing cases 0.

The 7 respondents who perceived there to be no problem were all from rural authorities.

(II) Homelessness policy

The next series of questions sought to ascertain if the authorities contacted held a written policy on homelessness, and if so, whether it distinguished separate groups. Whatever the current position may be, only 25 respondents were aware of their authority having a written policy on homelessness (see Table Two below); this figure represents only one third of the total sample. Housing authorities were thought to be slightly more likely than social work authorities to hold such a policy.

Table Two (a)

Does your authority have a written policy on homelessness?

	Social Work	Housing	Aggregate
Yes	10	15	25
No	27	23	50

Valid cases 75:   Missing cases 0.

Of the 25 respondents who claimed to have a 'written' policy, 20 stated that it distinguished the young single homeless from the homeless population in general. Those who stated that their policy made such a distinction were then asked if they made further distinctions. Whilst the numbers are small, Table Two (b) (overleaf) indicates that social work authorities were more likely to recognise a variety of groups amongst the young single homeless. This finding reflects the responsibilities that the social work department holds for particular 'vulnerable' groups among the young, rather than young single homeless people *per se*.

The research tested whether those authorities which held a written policy on homelessness were more likely to: engage in collaborative work with other agencies; hold joint assessment arrangements with another agency; have considered the relevance of community care working methods for the young homeless; and, have organised joint and/or specialised training for their staff. It was concluded that holding a written policy on homelessness did not influence the propensity of an authority to engage in any of the practice initiatives noted above.

Table Two (b)

Which groups amongst the young single homeless does it distinguish?

	Social Work (respondents = 9)	Housing (respondents = 11)	Aggregate
Previously in care	9	4	13
On supervision to children's hearings	4	1	5
On probation: after care	4	1	5
Young person with learning difficulties	4	1	5
Young person with mental health problems	5	2	7
Offenders or ex-offenders	4	1	5
Other	1	0	0

(N.B. Multiple choice question)

Valid cases 20:   Missing cases 0.

The fifty respondents who claimed that their authority held no written policy on homelessness were asked if they thought it would be helpful for them to have such a policy. Thirty-eight interviewees thought it would, and several were currently developing a policy statement. Most (36) believed that a general homelessness policy statement which included a discrete component for young people was desirable. Social work authorities were more likely to view a written policy on homelessness as a progressive step.

(III) The responsibility for formulating and implementing policy.

Tables Three (a) and (b) explore the related themes of the formulation and implementation of a youth homelessness policy. The evidence appears to overwhelmingly indicate that housing authorities should play the key role. Seventy-three interviewees believed that housing authorities should be primarily responsible for *formulating* policy, and 74 believed that housing authorities should be primarily responsible for *implementing* that policy.

Table Three

Which public services should be mainly responsible for
(a) formulating policy on youth homelessness?

	Housing	Social Work	Aggregate
Social Work	0	1	1
Housing	38	35	73
Other	0	1	1

Valid cases 75:   Missing cases 0.

(b) Implementing policy on youth homelessness?

	Housing	Social Work	Aggregate
Social Work	0	1	1
Housing	38	36	74
Other	0	0	0

Valid cases 75:   Missing cases 0.

These figures, however, hide an extremely common response to both these questions. Most respondents were uncomfortable at having to recommend a single agency to take the sole responsibility for both formulating and implementing policy. Fifty-five respondents felt that housing and social work should hold a *joint* responsibility in both respects. This group comprised of most social work authorities, and a significant number of housing authorities. In addition, many respondents believed that housing associations (voluntary agencies), Scottish Homes and the Scottish Office should all participate in this process.

(IV) Collaboration

The survey then turned to investigate whether any collaborative work is undertaken in response to the problem of homelessness. Table Four (a) shows that the majority (48) of respondents report meetings with other agencies in order to develop and/or implement policy for the homeless. It appears that social work and housing authorities are equally likely to have experience of collaborative ventures. (This result is not unexpected due to the matching of interview targets.)

Table Four (a)

In your area, do agency groups meet to develop and implement policies for the homeless?

	Social Work	Housing	Aggregate
Yes	24	24	48
No	13	14	27

Valid cases 75:   Missing cases 0.

These meetings (Table Four (b)) typically included housing and social work representatives, with voluntary organisations (usually housing associations) also being frequent contributors. The Health Board and the DSS were rarely included, and those respondents who noted an 'other' participating agency commonly referred to a specialist organisation in their locality. It was also noted that meetings were held on both a regular and *ad hoc* basis according to the issue of discussion.

Table Four (b)

Which agencies participate?

	Social Work	Housing
Housing	21	–
Social Work	–	21
DSS	1	2
Health Board	3	5
Voluntary	13	14
Other	7	8

(N.B. Multiple choice question)
Valid cases 48:   Missing cases 0.

Just over half of those interviewed believed that existing liaison arrangements were satisfactory, housing and social work staff reporting similar levels of satisfaction (Table Four (c) below).

Table Four (c)

Are liaison arrangements satisfactory?

	Social Work	Housing	Aggregate
Yes	19	21	40
No	18	17	35

Valid cases 75:   Missing cases 0.

Interviewees were further questioned as to whether elected members were involved in the development and implementation of policies for the homeless. Table Four (d) below indicates that social work respondents were more likely to come into contact with elected members in this respect, due in part to the range of client groups they recognise, but primarily because of the social work department's need to negotiate its regional responsibilities with a number of district authorities.

Table Four (d)

Do elected members play a part?

	Social Work	Housing	Aggregate
Yes	16	11	27
No	9	20	29

Valid cases 56:   Missing cases 19.

(V) Assessment arrangements

Approximately half of those interviewed (35) reported joint assessment arrangements with another agency (see Table Five (a) below). Social work authorities were only slightly more likely than housing authorities to engage in such practice. On the whole, these arrangements were held primarily between housing and social work authorities. Social work authorities, however, were more likely to involve other organisations, such as housing associations, specialist voluntary organisations, and health boards.

This was interpreted as being related to the responsibilities that social work authorities hold for a wide range of special need groups.

Table Five (a)

Do you have joint assessment arrangements with any other agency?

	Social Work	Housing	Aggregate
Yes	19	16	35
No	18	22	40

Valid cases 75:   Missing cases 0.

Social work authorities were also asked whether their plans for assessment and care management would be relevant to working with young homeless people.

Table Five (b)

Are plans for emergency assessment and care management relevant to working with young homeless people?

Yes	16
No	14

Valid cases 30:   Missing cases 7.

The respondents were almost equally divided between those who felt that community care methods of working were and were not applicable to the young homeless. The seven respondents who felt unable to answer, stated that their plans were still in the process of development.

Table Five (c)

If yes, are they?

Highly relevant	6
Moderately relevant	6
Minimally relevant	4

Valid cases 16:   Missing cases 0.

Of the 16 who said that their emergency plans were relevant there was a mixed response as to how relevant these were to the young homeless. In general, respondents noted the potential value of community care methods of working for priority categories amongst the young, but remained unsure as to whether community care responsibilities should be extended to incorporate young homeless people as a group in themselves. This is clearly an issue which requires a policy steer. If it is intended that the young homeless are most appropriately dealt with by community care methods of working, this should be communicated to the social work profession.

Housing authorities in turn were questioned about the need for further clarification of their responsibilities towards young people above that already defined in law and guidance. Twenty-three respondents affirmed such a need (see Table Five (d) below) mainly because they felt that uncertainties still remain as to what priority should be given to young people in need.

Table Five (d)

A need for further clarification?

Yes	23
No	14

Valid cases 37:   Missing cases 1.

The housing authorities were further questioned as to whether they would place any restrictions upon the rehousing of young people, and 30 respondents stated that they would *not*. Of the remainder, allocation was dependent upon the availability of appropriate accommodation or the young person's standing in relation to the homeless person's legislation.

(VI) Training

The next section of the survey considered the issue of training. Table Six (a) (below) reports on arrangements for joint training. Only 19 of the 75 respondents said that any such arrangements existed, and a relatively similar split between social work and housing can be discerned.

Table Six (a)

Do you have joint training arrangements with any other agencies?

	Social Work	Housing	Aggregate
Yes	11	8	19
No	26	30	56

Valid cases 75:   Missing cases 0.

The respondents were then asked whether any specialised training was organised for agency staff, either on work with regard to young people or homelessness. The results reflect the differing statutory responsibilities of each agency and it is clear that social work agencies are the main providers of training for work with young people, while housing agencies take the lead on training for work with the homeless.

Table Six (b)

Do your staff receive specialised training with regard to:
Young people?

	Social Work	Housing	Aggregate
Yes	30	7	37
No	7	31	38

Valid cases 75:   Missing cases 0.

Table Six (c)

Homelessness?

	Social Work	Housing	Aggregate
Yes	7	31	38
No	30	7	37

Valid cases 75: Missing cases 0.

Of those who offered specialised training, housing authorities used courses organised by the Institute of Housing and were particularly concerned with the interpretation of the housing legislation, and to a lesser extent young people's welfare rights. Social work authorities focused upon developing workers' skills acquired through basic training and concentrated on issues associated with preparation for independent living, particularly for those leaving care.

(VII) Social work tasks and performance

Tables Seven (a), (b) and (c) (below) explore the tasks undertaken in current social work practice. Respondents were asked to rank a range of social work tasks in order of importance, 1 being the most important, through to 8, being the least important. Column 1 records the number of respondents who identified each task as the most important in current practice. Assessment of vulnerability is clearly considered to be the most important task undertaken. No other single task is regarded as being even nearly as important and it is necessary to concentrate on column 2 (mean scores) to rank the remainder of the tasks. Information giving and advice followed by preparation for independent living are regarded as the second and third most important social work tasks. These are followed by advocacy and the strengthening of support networks.

Table Seven (a)

What do you see are the main jobs that the Social Work Services undertake, in current practice, in helping young homeless people?

	Most Important (frequency)	Mean Score
Preparation for independent living	4	3.3
Assessment of vulnerability	20	1.8
Information giving and advice	5	3.1
Strengthening of support networks	2	4.2
Advocacy (including liaison with other agencies)	2	4.1
Outreach work	0	6.5
Supervision (on grounds of risk: ex-offending)	2	5.6
Other (9 responses only)	2	6.8
Total	37	

Valid cases 37:   Missing cases 0.

Respondents were then asked to report how successful they thought their authority was in achieving these tasks (Table Seven (b)). The figures in each row show how 36 respondents voted: the last figure shows the average scored for each task.

Table Seven (b)

A successful completion of tasks?

	(1)	(2)	(3)	(4)	Mean
Preparation for independent living	4	19	9	4	2.4
Assessment of vulnerability	9	26	1	0	1.8
Information giving and advice	14	18	4	0	1.7
Strengthening of support networks	1	14	20	1	2.6
Advocacy (including liaison with other agencies)	4	25	6	1	2.1
Outreach work	1	7	16	12	3.1
Supervision (on the grounds of risk)	4	21	8	3	2.3
Other (9 responses)	1	4	2	2	–

Notes: 1 = very successful
         2 = quite successful
         3 = not very successful
         4 = unsuccessful

Valid cases 36:   Missing case 1.

The majority of respondents considered that they were reasonably successful in completing all tasks. The only exceptions were the strengthening of support networks and outreach work. Here the majority of respondents felt that they were 'not very successful' or 'unsuccessful' in completing these tasks, due in part to the limited resources.

Table Seven (c) overleaf reports the main tasks that the social work services undertake which contribute to the prevention of youth homeless.

Table Seven (c)

What steps do the social work authorities undertake to prevent young people from becoming homeless?

	Frequency
The development of appropriate care structures for adolescents in (and after) care	35
Counselling and support for young people and their carers	32
Case work with vulnerable families	31
Planning with housing providers to develop accommodation for young people	29
Advice and assistance, and out-of-hours crisis management	29
Group work and group activities for young people (after care)	23
Statutory work with offenders	18
Financial support to voluntary organisations providing supported accommodation	16

Valid cases 37:   Missing cases 0.

The most commonly cited categories relate to the tasks undertaken by social work authorities at an operational level, with young people both in care and from a care background. These included the development of care structures, counselling and support services, and group work. At strategic level, both the planning and funding of supported accommodation were identified as key tasks which address the prevention of youth homelessness.

(VIII) Improving the chances of young people

Finally, the survey turned to evaluate respondent perceptions as to what developments would make the most effective contribution towards preventing homelessness amongst young people (Table Eight (a) below). The categories were derived from data collected during an earlier stage of the research programme. It is clear that housing and social work authorities agree about the importance of each category. Forty-one out of 74 respondents thought that a more plentiful supply of housing for single people would make the most effective contribution. Seventeen felt that more generous social security payments would be more effective, yet most ranked this category as the second most important change. Closer collaboration between housing and social work authorities, and more and better trained social workers were seen as less likely to make an effective contribution. However, respondents were keen to stress that such developments were important. Their effectiveness would, however, be largely determined by the nature of the housing market and the generosity of the social security system.

Table Eight (a)

Which of the following developments would make the most effective contributions to preventing homelessness amongst young people?

		Importance Frequency				
		1	2	3	4	5
More plentiful supply of housing for single people	Housing	21	9	5	3	0
	Social Work	20	10	4	2	0
More generous social security for young people	Housing	8	18	9	2	1
	Social Work	9	15	9	2	1
More sensitive and better trained social workers for young people	Housing	0	2	6	16	14
	Social Work	0	1	1	16	18
Closer collaboration between Housing and Social Work Services	Housing	4	2	12	15	5
	Social Work	1	6	16	13	0
Other	Housing	5	7	6	2	6 (12)
	Social Work	6	4	5	4	2 (15)

Note: 1 = most important, 5 = least important

Valid cases (Housing) 38:   Missing cases 0.

Valid cases (Social Work) 36:   Missing cases 1.

In many instances, interviewees recommended additional developments which would also address the problem of preventing homelessness amongst young people. By far the most common response was a 'more plentiful supply of housing for single people'. Respondents argued the need for an increased provision and a greater diversity of 'supported' accommodation. Also commonly expressed was the need for 'greater educational inputs on the reality of independent living' and the 'strengthening of support networks for those leaving care'.

Conclusions

The most significant findings are:–

(i)   In urban areas, social workers and housing officers agree that there are severe housing problems for young people.

(ii)   Both social workers and those from housing departments felt that the lead role for formulating and implementing policy should be taken by Housing.

(iii)   Most people agreed that it would be helpful if their authority had a written policy on homelessness.

(iv)   However, holding a written policy on homelessness did not influence an authority's propensity to engage in a range of practice initiatives.

(v)   Around half of those questioned, from housing and social work, felt that existing liaison arrangements were unsatisfactory.

(vi)   Joint assessment between housing and social work is the exception rather than the rule.

(vii)   Only a minority of social workers – though a large one – regard community care methods of working as being relevant to the young homeless.

(viii) Only a minority of respondents reported opportunities for joint training between social workers and housing staff.

(ix)   Almost all social workers felt that assessment of vulnerability was the most important social work task in work with the young homeless.

(x)   There is clear agreement in both services about the priorities for policy in this field: first, a more plentiful supply of housing for young, single people, and second, more generous social security benefits for them.

(xi)   Better social work, and better training are thought to be important too, as a next priority.

Part III. Conclusions

Chapter 7

Conclusions

Introduction

This Chapter begins with a summary of the main things we have learnt about homeless young people in Scotland and the services they depend on: the trends, the reasons for them, the response which the community has made to their needs, and the defects of the present system of public services.

We then outline the strategic requirements for any attempt to put things right: the basic obligations of the State in this field, the main agencies and levels of government involved, and the principles on which they should collaborate. This section includes our main recommendations for housing and Social Security – services which go so far to shape the environment within which the social work services operate that they largely determine how successful social work can be.

Then we discuss the lessons to be learnt from London's experience, both for Scotland and for homeless Scots in London. Finally we review the law in this field and identify features of this system which need to be re-appraised if services for homeless young people are to be improved.

Together, these pages summarise our findings and set the scene for our main task which is to make recommendations for social workers and the services in which they operate. Those recommendations appear in our final Chapter.

Conclusions

In Chapter 1 we described the normal process of leaving home and showed that it depends on a balance between the "push" factors that encourage youngsters to leave their parents, the "pull" factors that attract them out, and the "support" factors that help them to make the transition. They are most likely to succeed if they take the various transitions they are making in the right order: first gaining sufficient maturity, education and training: then gaining a reasonably secure job and adequate earnings; then finding both a decent home (often after long periods in smaller, less secure, transitional forms of housing) and a supportive relationship with a life partner – educated and capable of earning a reasonable wage, like themselves – and only after that starting a new family. Those who make these transitions in other orders – having to abandon the shelter of parents before completing their education, to find shelter before earning a decent wage, or starting a family with no secure home or partner – have a much harder time. Then, if they do not have a supportive family to take refuge with when things go wrong, they are likely to become homeless.

We showed that for many youngsters the push factors, impelling them to leave home, have been sharpened while opportunities for housing, work and, if work fails, for social security payments – the support factors – have been weakened. Thus more of them than hitherto embark on these transitions too soon, ill-prepared, unsupported and in the wrong order. It is not surprising that the numbers of teenagers in public care rose sharply in the 'seventies and early 'eighties, and the increase in the numbers of homeless youngsters followed soon after.

Most of the young people we interviewed, as we showed in Chapter 2, are not tempted to leave their parents' homes by easy opportunities for housing, generous social security payments or irresponsible ignorance of the difficulties they will face. Nor can they readily return to their families. Indeed, many no longer have a family. Reluctant though they were to set forth on their own and desperately hard though their experience has often been, they decided to fend for themselves for what still seem to them very good reasons. Their experiences have made some of them difficult people to get on with, but many of those whom we met were remarkably resolute and resourceful. It follows that very few of these youngsters will be persuaded or compelled to return to their parents by frightening stories of the hardships of the homeless, or by policies which make it still more difficult for them to survive independently – although more of them may thereby end up in expensive prisons and hospitals.

No one foresaw the huge increase which has in recent years taken place in homelessness among young people and the public services were therefore ill-prepared by their powers, resources and training to respond to it. These services have not been organised with an appreciation of the processes – outlined in Chapter 1 – which normally enable young people to set up home independently, so they are ill-equipped to provide the support a normal family offers for youngsters who do not come from families of this kind. Chapter 3 reviewed recent changes in policies for housing and social security – changes which make life harder for homeless youngsters. It also showed the vagueness of social work duties towards this group. It argued for clarification and strengthening of social work responsibilities. It also suggested inclusion of the young homeless in Community Care legislation and planning, and called for a reappraisal of cash benefits for young people.

The current confusion about responsibilities for the young homeless was illustrated in Chapter 6 which reported the findings of our survey of experienced opinion in social work and housing authorities. While most of our respondents agreed that the lead role in formulating and implementing policy should be taken by housing departments they also agreed that social work services should be closely involved throughout in making these plans. Around half felt that existing liaison arrangements between housing and social work were unsatisfactory. The survey showed that joint assessment of young people's needs between housing and social work was the exception rather than the rule, as were opportunities for joint training of their staff.

There was clear agreement among both social work and housing staff that the first priority for any programme to improve services for homeless young people should be more housing for them, and the second priority should be more generous social security benefits. Closer collaboration between social work and housing services ranked third.

Chapters 4 to 6 deal with the social work response to youth homelessness, and since these chapters contain the bulk of the research-based evidence, it is worth summarising the major findings at greater length.

The major conclusion of Chapter 4, which analysed social work responses to four hypothetical cases, was the arbitrariness of professional decision-making. The level of consensus between workers, even those in the same team, was extremely low. For each of the hypothetical examples the chances of being taken on as a "case" depended more on the agency approached than on the "facts". It was clear from the transcripts that the "facts" had to be interpreted and the interpretations were influenced by presumptions about statutory responsibilities and the young people's motives, the extent of vulnerability, the resources available and the likelihood of success. The variability of professional decision-making stemmed from the poor definition of social work responsibilities (examined in Chapter 3) but it is relevant that the lack of professional consensus was particularly marked in area teams – the "front line" of the social work services.

The differences between the nature of the social work response in area and specialist teams was explored in more detail in Chapter 5. From the analysis of 80 "live" cases it was apparent that those managed by specialist teams were more likely to receive needs-led assessment, work on behavioural problems and training for life skills. By contrast, case management in area teams was often a reactive response to crisis and almost exclusively concerned with accommodation and benefits. These practice differences were shown to be rooted in resource inequalities. In area teams young homeless people compete for the social worker's time with all other client groups. In specialist teams they are the workers' main concern. And these workers, may have greater control over their case-loads and be less likely to get over-loaded.

Chapter 5 also identified three fundamental features of social work with young homeless people. First, the great majority of those who sought help from social work had had previous contact. They had histories and reputations. Second, their current lifestyles were highly volatile. Even over a 3 month period there were dramatic changes in their accommodation, relationships and personal circumstances. Third, most were "difficult" clients. They missed appointments, failed to carry out agreed courses of action and they often changed their minds suddenly and for seemingly inexplicable reasons.

Having summarised our main findings about clients it remains to demonstrate their inter-dependence. That young homeless people are suspicious of social workers and that social workers define them as "difficult" clients must be seen as two sides of the same coin. Similarly the fact that many encounters with social work present as an urgent crisis of some kind to staff who lack time and resources for a carefully considered response means that little more than advice and a bit of advocacy can be offered. This is directly related to the common view among young homeless people that social workers are ineffective. There is also an amplifying effect of these relationships which locks social workers and young people in a vicious circle of mutual distrust and despair. These processes are best represented diagrammatically, as follows:

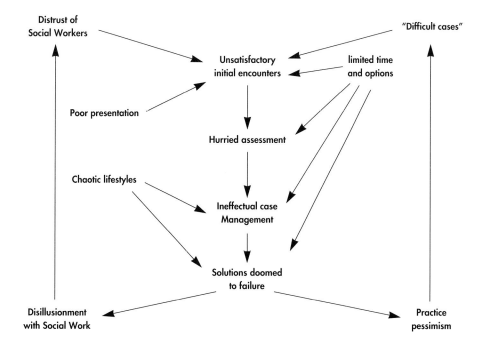

Unsatisfactory initial encounters are the result, on the one hand, of the young homeless person's distrust of social workers (normally stemming from a history of contact) and on the other of the social workers' definition of them as "difficult" cases (also a result of limited resources). This unsatisfactory initial encounter is unlikely to include an assessment of the young person's needs, but if it does, the assessment is likely to be hurried. Perfunctory assessment and case management is also affected by the social workers' lack of options and the clients' chaotic lifestyle. As a consequence, the services offered are often doomed to fail. When this occurs it reinforces the young person's disillusionment with social work and the social workers' predisposition to define young homeless people as difficult cases with a poor prognosis.

Similar vicious circles can be seen in the housing field. Vulnerable young people may be re-housed in forbidding neighbourhoods with scant support from anyone, under programmes which may be as much concerned with filling empty flats quickly as with meeting the youngsters' needs. As their stock of housing dwindles and the demands from single person households of all kinds increase, many housing authorities have difficulty in finding any space for homeless young people. Unsuitably placed and unsupported, the youngsters may then get into difficulties with the rent, the neighbours or the maintenance of their houses, and therefore lose their tenancies in circumstances which get them black-listed by housing authorities. They then have nowhere to turn for shelter and may end up in prison, or go south to London where things are harder still for them. Equally unhappy experiences of training and employment – and therefore, too, of the social security system – were also encountered in our research.

These patterns help to explain why we found that young people are so reluctant to seek help from the public services which were set up to protect them, and often approach these services reluctantly, suspiciously and too late.

In order to improve the response made by all services to the young homeless it is necessary to break this cycle. The recommendations which follow are directed towards this end.

Strategic requirements

Our main task is to offer advice to the social work services. But their experience, as we show in Chapter 6, is that the homeless cannot be effectively helped and social work cannot be effectively done until the people concerned are adequately and securely housed, and have an income sufficient to live on which meets their housing costs. Young homeless people are no exception to this rule. In this section we consider the strategic requirements which follow from it.

First we need to clarify the obligations of the State. Anyone aged 16 or over can set up home on their own if they can afford to do so. The State is only obliged to help them to do so if:

(1) it has previously taken over parental responsibilities for them, or

(2) they are young, vulnerable and unable to return safely to a home provided by their families, or

(3) it is in the interests of the community to enable them to leave home – to become students or trainees, for example – or

(4) because, as adults, they should have the same opportunities for entry to social rented housing or house purchase as everyone else.

It is the first two of these groups that we are concerned with. They are much the smallest of the four categories, but their needs were not foreseen and therefore pose critical problems for which the State is ill-prepared.

In some areas the role of the State has been confused by its own need to keep empty flats filled. This has led some housing authorities to offer young people council flats in unattractive places with no supporting services to help them. That should not happen: it is a policy for dealing with voids, not homelessness.

What further obligations does the State have towards young people whom it helps to house? A private landlord who has the right – indeed a business obligation – to exclude certain tenants because they seem likely to get behind with the rent, to damage the property or to make trouble with the neighbours has no other obligations. But local housing authorities and subsidised housing associations – "social landlords" – are often expected to house tenants whom the private landlord would regard as risky. That is one of the reasons for their existence.

Social landlords

It follows that social landlords have a duty to assess their tenants, to keep in touch with any who might be in difficulties, to keep track of what is going on, and to ensure that support services of appropriate kinds are available for those who need them. The costs involved are a necessary part of the operations of a social landlord, and provision should be made to cover them. It is beyond our terms of reference to say whether that should come through the housing revenue account and housing benefit payments to tenants, or from other sources such as the social work departments' community care budgets.

Support services do not necessarily have to be provided or paid for by the landlord. Social work, health, police and community education services have duties to provide many of them. But whoever provides them, the social landlord should ensure that such services are available, that tenants' needs for them are assessed and they are helped to make use of whatever support they need. To rehouse vulnerable people without ensuring that these things are done can lead to very destructive results for tenants and landlords – the kind of 'vicious circle' we have described. It is as irresponsible as building and letting a house without drains or a supply of clean water.

It will sometimes be clear that a tenant is likely to be vulnerable. It would be very surprising if a 16 year old did not need some help if he or she were without any family and setting up on their own for the first time in a neighbourhood where they knew no-one. But that vulnerability does not automatically end at the age of 18 or 20. Their needs will depend on many other things; whether they are healthy and socially mature; have a job, friends at work and enough money to go out and meet people; live in a secure and stable place with kindly neighbours; and so on. No simple formula can define the circumstances which signal vulnerability. They have to be assessed and a judgement made about them.

Many of these circumstances depend partly on the policy and practice of the landlord who decides where people are to live and may help to build up – or to undermine – the social stability of the area. The fact that social landlords can increase or reduce people's vulnerability through their own actions is another reason why they should take the lead in assessing it, and either providing whatever support is required or making sure that this support is available.

As social landlords adopt increasingly commercial practices, these requirements will call for a thoughtful meshing of business and welfare ethics. And as local housing authorities have to rely increasingly on housing associations to provide the houses their people need, closer collaboration between these agencies will be called for.

Social work

But if housing authorities must take the lead in ensuring that these assessment and support services are available, social work authorities must be involved at every stage in planning for these services and providing them. They already provide such services for many potentially vulnerable tenants: those under the age of 18 who have been in their care; those who have illnesses or handicaps, physical or mental; and those with children. These obligations and powers should be extended to cover all who are homeless or in danger of becoming so, and are assessed as being vulnerable. If nothing is done for them, many of these people are likely to end up in hospitals, prisons or other forms of residential care provided at great expense by the State. Homelessness also makes it impossible for people to get training and jobs, and that, too, ultimately makes them dependent on the State.

It is at the moment unclear whether the Community Care Plans which the social work authorities are preparing should make any provision for such people unless they fall into one of the categories listed in the previous paragraph. Their right to assessment and community care services and the authorities' right to secure funds for this purpose from their Community Care budgets should be made clear.

To combine housing and social work services effectively will call for policy decisions and planning procedures at central, regional and district levels of government, and it is to these that we now turn.

Joint planning

The aim of policy should be to prevent homelessness and institutionalisation among young people. An objective as important and difficult as this will call for authoritative decisions by Ministers, leading to a requirement that similar written policy commitments be promulgated by councils at regional and district levels. Although homelessness is more commonly found in the cities – often because homeless youngsters go, or are sent, there from other places – the family problems which give rise to it are found everywhere. Thus whatever new policies are adopted should apply everywhere in Scotland, although they will not call for major resources in small towns and rural areas. It is only in the bigger cities that the more elaborate responses will be needed.

Some continuing working group will be needed at the centre to oversee and implement these policies. In addition to officials responsible for housing, the voluntary housing movement and social work, close consultation should be maintained with the services responsible for social security, education and prisons, along with voluntary agencies working with young people in these fields – probably represented by the Scottish Council for the Single Homeless.

Among the main instruments for implementing these policies will be the Community Care and Housing Plans of local authorities. It should be made clear that both should show how these authorities intend to provide for the needs of young people who are homeless or in danger of becoming homeless, what resources will be devoted to this work, and how the two authorities intend to collaborate for this purpose. The roles of housing associations funded by Scottish Homes and of other voluntary agencies should also be made clear, but these will vary from place to place in ways which depend on the local resources available.

It will take time to meet these needs. More, or different, staff, more training, more housing or different housing will all be required – though not in all places. To make sustained progress will call for reliable information about the numbers, character and needs of young homeless people, and about the housing and other services dealing with them. None of this is yet available. Effective planning to meet these needs will therefore call for official investigation and statistical monitoring to ensure that progress is being made and the public services are not again overtaken by unforeseen social trends.

Providing housing and support services for the more vulnerable homeless young people will be of little use unless they can afford to pay whatever it costs to survive decently. That will call for changes in their rights to income support, grants and loans from the social fund, and housing benefit. These financial benefits can be provided in various combinations and in more or less selective ways. The more selective they are, the heavier the staff costs and the poorer the rates of take-up will be. It would lead us beyond our terms of reference to make detailed recommendations about these provisions, but we briefly outline the issues which will have to be considered in the last section of this Chapter.

Lessons from London

We interviewed young Scots in a London hostel which specialises in helping this group, and reported on their composition and experience at the end of Chapter 2. We also did our best, with the help of local experts, to learn more general lessons from those working to help homeless young people in London. These are the main conclusions we draw from this evidence.

Scotland has much to learn from the ways in which the Irish have responded to the needs of their own young migrants. The search for work in foreign countries has been for so long a necessary part of that under-employed economy's culture that the Government, the Church and voluntary agencies have joined forces to:

(i)   provide guidance for young people who may be emigrating;
(ii) develop hostels and housing for young people in London and other cities through housing associations funded by the British Government;
(iii) set up social centres where emigrants of all ages can meet and keep in touch with home;
(iv) help youngsters find jobs and training; and
(v) provide help for those who wish to return home.

Scottish needs may not be thought to justify quite so elaborate a programme, but our evidence shows that young Scots who become homeless in London feel themselves to be exposed to much the same indifference and hostility that foreigners experience in a strange city. Irish practice should be studied in consultation with "Borderline", the admirable but small-scale project for young Scots set up in London by the Church of Scotland.

It was clear that most of the young Scots we met in London did not intend to return to Scotland if they could avoid it. But it was also clear that they had come to a city where the ratios of jobs to vacancies and of wage levels to rents are particularly punishing. If advice is to be provided in Scotland for youngsters contemplating emigration – and we understand the Scottish Office is currently commissioning a study for this purpose – it should include information about other cities in various parts of the UK where these ratios offer youngsters more favourable opportunities.

The young Scots we met said they would have found their first arrival in London much easier if there had been information points at rail and bus stations receiving travellers from Scotland where up-to-date information about accommodation for newcomers such as hostel vacancies and their locations could be found. We understand that SHAC – the Shelter Housing Action Centre – is currently developing a service of this kind with the support of the Department of the

Environment. This experiment should be carefully followed, both for the help it may give young Scots in London and for the model it may offer for replication in the larger Scottish cities.

London, along with several other English cities, has enterprising examples of publicly funded voluntary projects, operating on a core-and-cluster basis, which offer many different kinds of aid for homeless youngsters, ranging from soup and sandwiches to housing, counselling and help in rebuilding relationships with families. Some, too, give special attention to medical and psychiatric needs. Scottish agencies, statutory and voluntary, working in this field should be encouraged to keep in touch with these projects and to exchange experience with them.

This account of lessons to be learnt from London would not be complete if it did not also include some warnings. In a city with greater housing shortages and a bigger flow of inward migrants than any to be found in Scotland it is perhaps natural that publicly funded voluntary organisations have generally taken the lead in helping the homeless. For some youngsters this pattern is beginning to create a hierarchy which virtually compels them to live at first on the street, then to move into emergency shelter of various kinds, then to temporary supported housing projects, followed by a furnished tenancy, before securing the mainstream housing they wanted in the first place. Scottish cities, with a public housing stock that is more plentiful in relation to needs, should recognise that this long trail may be more a response to London's harsh necessities than to the needs of the homeless.

The legal agenda

Social work, we have repeatedly found, cannot be effective unless it operates within an effective structure of supporting services – particularly in the fields of housing and social security. Social workers and housing managers confirm this finding: their first priorities for helping young homeless people are an improvement in these two services. This has compelled us to look beyond the social work services which are the central concern of our brief and to make recommendations about the strategic framework within which they function before dealing with their operations. Turning now to consider the legal implications of our recommendations we briefly list the main questions to be considered, rather than proposing detailed changes in the law. To go further would take us well beyond our terms of reference.

As Chapter 3 made clear, this agenda springs from the fact that the growth of homelessness among young people is a recent and wholly unforeseen phenomenon which our legal system was not prepared for. Since there is no sign that homelessness among the young will disappear – all the factors which brought about the increase are likely to continue for many years – the sooner this agenda can be purposefully tackled, the better.

We discuss each of the three main fields in turn, adopting the order of priority given us by those interviewed in our national survey: housing, social security, and social work.

Housing

Housing authorities are required to submit Housing Plans to the Scottish Office Environment Department every four years – Glasgow does so every two years. The statistical returns they make every year to the Department incorporate figures for homelessness, broken down by broad age groups and household types. But their Plans are not required to make any special provision for homelessness – though many of them in practice do – or to deal specifically with the young homeless.

Housing authorities have been sent literature on the new provisions for community care, but this, too, makes no reference to young homeless people. They are required to show that they are working in partnership with other agencies, but those requirements deal mainly with housing associations, private builders and developers – not with the social work and voluntary agencies whose help is likely to be needed for young homeless people.

The authorities' general responsibilities for the homeless hinge – as we showed in Chapter 3 – on the concepts of "homelessness", "priority need", "intentionality" and "local connection". The basic problem for young people is the uncertainty about the priority to be accorded to them. Some authorities use this uncertainty in generous ways. But in many, owing to lack of resources or to policy decisions, these four requirements become hurdles for homeless youngsters to surmount. If they do not fall at one, they are likely to be floored by the next. The weakness of the position of these youngsters is exacerbated by the fact that they have no formal rights of appeal.

All these points need to be reconsidered. Some can be dealt with in circulars and codes of guidance. Others will call for changes in the law. A central requirement will be the development of a more comprehensive and reliable concept of "vulnerability" which applies to young people and ensures priority for those who need it. Some forms of vulnerability are already recognised – exposure to financial or sexual exploitation for example. To develop the concept more extensively and humanely will call for judgements based on proper assessment procedures in which social workers will often have to be involved. It cannot be defined in some merely mechanical legal fashion.

Cash benefits

In the housing field we are dealing with a system which has been developed in more generous ways – particularly after the 1977 Act – but without foreseeing that young people would emerge as being in urgent need of its help. In the field of cash benefits, however, we are dealing with systems which were in 1988 deliberately made much less generous towards young people on the assumption that if benefits were withdrawn either they would get jobs and support themselves, or their families would care for them. Our research and the experience of all who work with homeless youngsters shows that while, for the more fortunate, this assumption may be valid, for most of the homeless it is mistaken. It has to be re-examined if their needs are to be met.

These are some of the main questions which will have to be considered. Should the exclusion of 16 and 17 year olds from Income Support (IS) and the provision of IS at the lower rate for those aged 18 to 24 be reversed? Or should they be reversed only for those unable to live at home? What influence would the latter policy exert on families in which parents are already tempted to throw out youngsters who may be very difficult to live with?

If young people are offered unfurnished housing, should they be given help to furnish it from the Social Fund – now virtually unavailable to them? If not, should the landlords of social housing be obliged to provide more furnished housing? And, if so, how should charges for furniture, kitchen equipment and related services be treated for Housing Benefit purposes?

Housing Benefit is now withdrawn at a very rapid rate when recipients start earning money – particularly for those in expensive, furnished accommodation. The resulting poverty trap makes it very difficult for low-paid youngsters to accept jobs. Community Charge has exacerbated this problem. The "junior rate" of Housing Benefit paid to those aged under 25 makes things harder still for them.

IS and Housing Benefit were originally intended to meet housing and financial needs. To wield them in ways designed to punish younger people is confusing, destructive and – many would say – unfair.

Social work services

The law of social work is less clearly defined than that of the other services we have considered and in the child care and community care fields it is currently under review. Here we are contributing to debates which are already under way. These debates should resolve three closely related questions.

(1) Social work authorities have a general duty "to promote social welfare" and help "persons in need" (Social Work (Scotland) Act 1968, Part II) but it is not clear whether young homeless people are entitled to services under either provision. Our study shows that they should be. But it also shows that most young people manage very well without help from social workers, and many others who may need such help are unwilling to accept it. Thus it should be made clear that young people who are homeless or likely to become homeless and deemed to be vulnerable are entitled to help, and that the Social Work Service has a duty to offer this help. Identifying who is to get this help will call for judgements based on assessments which the service should be equipped to make.

(2) It should also be made clear that these young people – vulnerable and homeless, or threatened with homelessness – are entitled to assessment and care under the Community Care Plans to be introduced in April 1993, along with the other far larger groups for which these Plans are being devised. The social work authorities must therefore be entitled to use their community care budgets for this purpose. The aim of this service for the homeless is to reintegrate them into the mainstream of society and to prevent institutionalisation and human suffering, just as it is when community care is provided for others, such as the old, and people with mental illnesses or handicaps, under the NHS and Community Care Act, 1990.

It follows that the Community Care Plans now being prepared should make specific provision for this group, and should show that the service is collaborating with housing authorities, and voluntary social work and housing agencies for this purpose.

(3) There are very few legal requirements governing after care for young people who have been in the care of local authorities. These need to be clarified and strengthened. We have shown that a large proportion of the homeless youngsters – and particularly of those whom the social work authorities find most difficult to deal with – have previously been in care.

The Child Care Law Review has already proposed that responsibilities of this kind to be found in the 1968 Act should be strengthened, and that local authorities should have a duty to prepare these youngsters for independent living before they leave their care. Our findings support those recommendations. However, much of the agenda we have identified in the social work field can be tackled without fresh legislation if Ministers are convinced that it should be.

Conclusion

The legal system applying to homeless and potentially homeless young people is flawed at many points in all the public services concerned. That is because these youngsters have emerged as the victims of unforeseen economic and social changes, exacerbated in some cases by policy changes based on a misunderstanding of current social trends. Now that we have a better grasp of what is going on, the law and its interpretation must be changed to provide a more effective response. The numbers of homeless young people, when compared with those in the other groups whom these services deal with, are tiny. But their needs are urgent – and if left unmet, ultimately expensive for all of us.

Chapter 8

Recommendations For Social Work Services

We come now to our recommendations for the social work services. These we present under the four headings provided by our brief: (a) preventive action, (b) assistance at the time of initial enquiry, (c) emergency liaison, and (d) supportive accommodation and services.

(a) Preventive action

1. In all study areas social workers noted that many clients were unprepared for independent living. Social workers and housing experts should collaborate with educationalists to design an Independent Living module for inclusion in Modern Studies teaching.
    (ACTION by Departments of Social Work, Housing and Education)

2. The research has shown that many young people only present in crisis situations. Social workers should collaborate with teachers under arrangements agreed with their local education and community education departments to develop more sensitive 'triggers' to identify those young people who may be experiencing problems in the home. This should include joint planning initiatives, including the use of outreach workers, to provide accessible information for all young people at school and in the neighbourhood. This information should outline both the formal and the informal advice and assistance available to them, and the dangers of leaving home without making adequate preparations.
    (ACTION by Departments of Social Work and Education)

3. The research identified a number of examples of good practice in mediation and reconciliation. Social Work Departments should encourage and support agencies which offer a mediation service for parents and children who are experiencing difficulties. As well as providing a counselling component, this should also include short term respite accommodation for young people, in order to relieve pressure at home. Our research indicates that such programmes are particularly successful for those under 16 years of age.
    (ACTION by Social Work Departments and Voluntary Organisations)
    Specialist team (G) referred to in Chapter 5 provides a good example of this kind of approach. The work of this project deserves to be better known and replicated in other settings.

4. The research identified a widespread reluctance among young people to seek help from statutory agencies. Social work departments should collaborate with statutory and voluntary agencies to provide informal drop-in centres. They should be staffed by workers skilled in dealing with young people and expert in providing 'fastlane' access to resources where appropriate. Such centres would have the additional function of monitoring prevalence and trends in the homeless population.
    (ACTION by Social Work, Housing and Voluntary Organisations)

5. All four of the developments proposed above – and particularly those for counselling services and drop-in centres – should involve young people who have recently been homeless, offering some of them training through YTS and other schemes, and recruiting them to paid jobs in these projects. We have repeatedly been told by young people passing through difficult times

that they have been suspicious of officials but found that other youngsters who have had similar experiences gave them the best support and advice.
(ACTION by Social Work)

6. Workers in all agencies commented on the lack of shared training opportunities. Joint training arrangements for work with young homeless people should be developed between housing, social work and voluntary agencies. Young people who have experienced homelessness should contribute to this training.
(ACTION by Scottish Office Social Work Services Group to provide training funds)

(b) <u>Social work assistance at the time of "initial inquiry"</u>

1. A needs-led, rather than a service-led, standardised assessment process must be developed. This should be consistent with current developments in the assessment of groups entitled to community care and should speedily identify which agency is best placed to respond to the young person's needs. A two stage process is envisaged: a preliminary assessment by staff of the agency at the point of first contact, followed by speedy referral to the most appropriate case managing agency. This case manager would conduct a more thorough needs-led assessment, involving a review of the young person's social, physical and mental circumstances, existing and potential social support, motivation and long-term wants and needs. It is unlikely that such an assessment can be made on a single occasion; indeed, in the examples of good practice identified in Chapter 5, the best assessments 'evolved' over a number of meetings. It is also unlikely that such an assessment can be successfully conducted by staff with no experience of young homeless people. The evidence drawn from both the vignette data and the monitoring of live cases illustrates the difficulty of work with this client group. Most of the examples of good practice come from experienced workers in specialist teams. If case management is to be applied to the young homeless, it is in the specialist teams where the future case managers may be found.
(ACTION by Social Work)

2. In all settings, but particularly among inexperienced workers in urban settings, the research identified serious information gaps. In each of the large urban centres case-management would be facilitated by the introduction of a centralised data record. This facility would monitor changes in needs and resources irrespective of whether they can readily be identified as a single agency's responsibility. Its major function would be to monitor the day to day availability of city-wide services, including accommodation vacancies. Such a facility would be invaluable for the management of individual cases but its aggregate data would also provide essential information for keeping track of overall levels of need.
(ACTION by Social Work)

3. To combat the delays identified in all research settings, emergency care packages which can be "taken off the shelf" should be developed and made available to inexperienced workers. There are a number of specialist centres which could be commissioned to design these packages. An alternative or additional way of improving the practice of inexperienced workers would be to offer them support and advice through a programme of "young homelessness clinics" in area teams. Again, there are a number of specialist teams which could offer such a service.
(ACTION by Social Work)

(c) <u>Emergency liaison arrangements</u>

1. Our research shows that existing emergency liaison arrangements are often underdeveloped and confused, leading to considerable delays in providing an appropriate service to young people in crisis situations. It is recommended that representatives of all helping agencies, led by the housing and social work departments, meet to clarify responsibilities and local procedures.
    (ACTION by Social Work and Housing)
    The Glasgow Council for the Single Homeless, which represents political leaders and senior staff of all the relevant services – central and local, statutory and voluntary – coupled with a monthly Lunch Club of the field staff working with single homeless people provide a model. They have for many years helped to make this city one of the UK's leaders in this field of work.

2. A major requirement of all local emergency arrangements is a continually updated and comprehensive information system. The computerised data record system already recommended for each of the large urban centres would meet emergency as well as routine requests for accommodation. Its function and location should be made widely known to young people who may need its help.
    (ACTION by Social Work and Housing)

3. The needs of many young homeless people will not be met by emergency arrangements alone, no matter how efficient they may be, and cases dealt with in this way must be reviewed to identify those who may require subsequent assessment and help.
    (ACTION by Social Work)

(d) <u>The provision of supportive accommodation or support services</u>

Social work departments should not have their own stock of housing for use by the 16 to 20 year old age group, apart from temporary accommodation needed to help youngsters in their care who are preparing for independent living. Social workers would soon find that the management of a housing stock would conflict with their roles as advocates and counsellors. Instead, social work departments should promote:

1. The provision by statutory and voluntary agencies of a wide range of supported accommodation. Our case studies have identified several examples of good practice which should be developed. Examples include joint housing and social work initiatives at both strategic and operational levels, in which:
    (a) A housing department holds a number of furnished scatter flats;
    (b) all applicants under the age of 25 receive an assessment of their capacity for independent living;
    (c) young people's agreement is sought for an appropriate support package where necessary;
    (d) the social work department can make emergency referrals;
    (e) cases are managed by housing support workers and homemakers;
    (f) more intensive social work support can be introduced where appropriate; and
    (g) joint housing and social work training initiatives are established.
    (ACTION by Social Work and Housing)

2. Interviews with social workers and young people revealed the difficulties of securing adequate transitional arrangements. All hostels which provide emergency or short-term

accommodation for young people should also work to help them move into more permanent accommodation. Wherever agencies receive core social work department funding, this requirement should be specified in their grant conditions.
(ACTION by Social Work)

3. Where support services are linked to young people's benefit packages, gaining employment can deprive them of benefits and the support services which go with them. The continuance of support packages needs to be guaranteed at least in the short-term. Similar protection should be accorded to young people who gain employment while living in furnished accommodation for which rental demands may rise dramatically as they start earning some money. These requirements will call for an agreement about the rate at which benefit and support packages taper off.
(ACTION by Social Work and Social Security)

4. A recent study by the National Foster Care Association (reported in *The Independent* on May 7th, 1992) based on a survey of 200 foster parents, suggests that many of them continue to help youngsters who were in their care – paying for groceries and Community Charge and providing emotional support long after they leave their foster homes. There is a source of support among these foster parents which deserves to be more systematically mobilised and resourced.
(ACTION by Social Work)

Piloting the recommendations: an agenda for a demonstration project and action research.
Research-based recommendations require a period of development work before they can be generally applied. The proposals outlined above should be developed through one or two demonstration projects coupled with a programme of action research. The details of such projects and programmes go beyond our remit but the following elements are crucial:
(i)   an informal drop-in facility offering advice and assistance to young people facing difficulties at home.
(ii) a central location and independent identity having no overt connection with statutory agencies.
(iii) a helpline advice and counselling service drawing on the help of some recently homeless young people.
(iv) a remit to develop a needs-led assessments instrument, referral guidelines and emergency care packages for use in other agencies.
(v)   a remit to develop an on-line computerised record of day-to-day accommodation available in the district.

Some of these services are already provided in the settings we studied, and particularly in the specialist teams. But no single agency combines all of them. However, at least one of the specialist teams included in this study comes close to providing an optimal response to youth homelessness. Our final recommendation under this heading, therefore, is that a team of this sort should be strengthened and designated as a national demonstration project.
(ACTION by Scottish Office Social Work Services Group)

A note on costs and benefits

A complete costing of all the recommendations is beyond our brief and competence. Indeed, we are tempted to make the additional recommendation that an economist be commissioned to undertake a full appraisal of the cost of youth homelessness to the nation and a complete costing, both of our detailed recommendations and more general proposals. If such an appraisal were to be conducted, we suspect that the existing costs to the nation would greatly exceed those of our proposals for reform.

Restricting ourselves to the immediate and identifiable costs of our specific recommendations for social work services, we offer the following estimates:

(i)   to provide a centralised data record system for each of Scotland's major cities would incur capital costs of around £200K and yearly running costs of around £100K;

(ii)   to encourage and strengthen mediation services in each of Scotland's major cities we estimate a yearly expenditure of around £350K;

(iii) to provide informal drop-in centres in each of Scotland's cities would probably incur capital costs of around £400K and yearly running costs of around £240K;

(iv) Independent Living Modules, Information and Emergency Packs could be provided for an overall outlay of around £100K;

(v)   joint training courses for social workers and housing staff could be provided at a yearly cost of around £75K;

(vi) the proposed National Demonstration Project should ideally run for a minimum of three years, at an annual cost of around £100K. If two such projects were launched these costs would be doubled.

(vii) Associated research work, monitoring these developments and helping to improve them and disseminate the lessons to be learnt from them would involve additional costs which could, however, be met from other sources.

The overall cost of these recommendations we estimate to be of the order of £3.5 million over three years. For young homeless people and social workers struggling to meet their needs the benefits would be invaluable.

Appendices

1. Legal Notes

Young people seeking accommodation through the Homeless Persons' Legislation

1   Formerly statutory responsibility for homeless persons lay with local authority social work departments. Social work still has some limited duties as regards homelessness; these are discussed below.

2   These duties are in addition to the housing authorities general duty to give 'reasonable preference' to homeless people in the allocation of council housing (S20 of Housing (Scotland) Act 1987). However, this is a vague provision, and probably unenforceable other than in cases of the most blatant violation. It should also be noted that housing authorities are prohibited from discriminating on the basis of age both as regards admission to the housing list, and allocation of accommodation, provided the applicant has attained the age of 16 (S19(1) (a) and S20(2) (a) (iii) of the Housing (Scotland) Act 1987).

3   S37 of the Housing (Scotland) Act 1987. A revised Code of Guidance was issued in April 1991, and supersedes the one published in September 1980 under the 1977 Act.

4   In *Kelly and Mallon v. Monklands DC (1986 SLT 165)* the housing authority's decision was quashed on the grounds that it failed to have regard to certain recommendations in the Code of Guidance concerned with co-operation between housing and social work departments.

5   S28 of the 1987 Act.

6   Ibid S29.

7   Ibid S24.

8   Ibid S24 (2A) and (2B). These subsections were added by the Law Reform (Miscellaneous Provisions) (Scotland) Act 1990, to harmonise the law in Scotland with english law as regards 'reasonableness' criteria for housing to constitute 'accommodation' for the purposes of the homeless persons' legislation. The Code of Guidance (4.3.5) gives examples of the kinds of accommodation which may not be reasonable for a person to continue to occupy e.g. bed and breakfast hotels, housing below the 'tolerable' standard etc.

9   *Din v. Wandsworth LBC 1981 3 A11 ER 881.* This principle was applied to women's refuges in *R v. Ealing exp. Sidhu 1981 HLR 45,* and would apply to night shelters and other emergency accommodation young people may have access to.

10 S24 (3) (a) of 1987 Act.

11 S24 (3) (b) of 1987 Act. This provision will be of importance to young people who have left home because of violence or abuse. Such young people must be considered homeless even if their family is willing to provide them with accommodation, if they would be under threat of violence from another resident, or from someone with whom they previously resided, if they returned home.

12 S24 (3) (d) of the 1987 Act. Overcrowding is defined by S135 of the 1987 Act.

13 S24 (4).

14 S30 (4).

15 S25. The groups specified as having a 'priority need' for accommodation include pregnant women; persons with dependent children; persons who are homeless as the result of an emergency; and persons who are vulnerable as a result of old age, mental illness or handicap, physical disability or other special reason.

16   Code of Guidance 4.4.4.1. In *Kelly v. Monklands DC* (discussed below) it was held that a young person can be 'at risk' of sexual or financial exploitation even if the police have no evidence that such exploitation has ever occurred in the local authority area.

17   Code of Guidance 4.4.4.2.

18   Code of Guidance 4.4.4.4.

19   Code of Guidance 2.11.2. (See discussion of *Steventon* case below.)

20   Code of Guidance 4.4.4.

21   Scottish Office Central Research Unit Paper, "Homelessness in Scotland", George J. Duguid, published in September 1990.

22   Ibid. Page 23, paragraph 2.50.

23   Ibid. Page 24, paragraph 2.54.

24   See above Note 4.

25   [1987] GWD 15-576.

26   S31 (4). The Code of Guidance suggests various kinds of advice and assistance which may be appropriate, including advice on housing, financial, legal and social matters. (Code of Guidance 6.)

27   S26 (1).

28   Code of Guidance 4.5.5.

29   S26 (3). The Code of Guidance at 4.5.8 gives some examples of persons who may be regarded as unaware of relevant facts. In *Wincentzen v. Monklands DC 1988 SLT 259* the applicant was held not to be intentionally homeless as she was unaware of the relevant fact that her father would act on the threat which he had made to refuse to allow her to return home after staying with her mother and stepfather for the duration of a college course.

30   Code of Guidance 4.5.6.

31   S26 (4) Code of Guidance 4.5.6.

32   Code of Guidance 4.5.7.

33   Code of Guidance 4.5.9. However, an authority can take into account the reasons for the applicant leaving his last settled accommodation, even if he has lived in unsettled accommodation more recently.

34   Code of Guidance 4.5.11.

35   S26 (2) of the 1987 Act.

36   Ibid S31 (3).

37   Ibid S32 (3) (b).

38   Ibid S28 (2).

39   Ibid S27 (1).

40   Ibid S33.

41   Ibid S31 (2).

42   Ibid S32 (2).

43   Ibid S30 (4).

44   In *Kelly v. Monklands DC* (see above Note 4) the local authority failed to take into account relevant considerations regarding social work assessment of a 16 year old girl as 'vulnerable' for the purposes of the 'priority need' qualification.

45   In *Kelly v. Monklands* the court also held that the local authority had made a 'manifestly unreasonable' decision by deciding that a 16 year old girl with no income, no assets, and who had apparently left home because of violence, was not 'vulnerable'.

46   See "A Guide to Judicial Review in Scotland", by Tom Mullen, published by Shelter (Scotland) in 1987, for a fuller discussion of the grounds for judicial review.

47   "A Guide to Judicial Review in Scotland" (cited above) provides a full examination of the issues of law and procedure involved in judicial review actions generally, and homelessness applications in particular.

48   In the Scottish Office research paper "Homelessness in Scotland" (cited above Note 21), 42% of respondent local authorities stated that there was an appeals procedure for applicants within their authority; however only one of these local authorities automatically notified unsuccessful applicants in writing of this appeal, and only 6 did so verbally. It seems likely that the appeals systems referred to are not specific to homeless applicants, but are available to those affected by other types of local authority decisions, and that most homeless applicants will be unaware of the appeals mechanism unless the local authority informs them of it.

Cash benefits to young people

49   S14 (1) (a); (2) and 17 (1) (a) (i) of the Social Security Act 1975 as amended.

50   S20 (1) of the Social Security Act 1975 as amended.

51   S13 and Sch. 3 para. 1 and 3 of the Social Security Act 1975 as amended.

52   The Social Security Act 1986 fundamentally altered the structure of means tested benefits, and came into force in April 1988.

53   S20 (3) (a) of the Social Security Act 1986 as amended by the Social Security Act 1988 S4. Before 1988 the qualifying age was 16, and some 16 and 17 year olds continue to qualify (see below).

54   S20 (3) (c). If the claimant has a partner, he or she must also not be in full-time paid employment. The term the legislation uses is 'remunerative employment'. This was defined as work for 24 hours or more a week, being work for which payment was made or in expectation of payment [Regulation 5 of Income Support (General) Regulations 1987 (SI 1987 No. 1967)]. However from 7th April, 1992 full-time is redefined as 16 hours per week paid work. This will have serious consequences for persons in (previously) part-time work of between 16 and 24 hours a week who will lose their entitlement to IS.

55   S20 (3) (d) (ii). The term used is 'relevant education' and is defined in Regulation 12 (SI 1987 No. 1967). This provision is basically concerned with persons who are receiving full time non-advanced education. Regulation 13 lists persons who are eligible for IS notwithstanding the fact they are receiving relevant education.

56   S20 (3) (d) (ii). Persons not required to be available for work are listed in Regulation 8; persons treated as available for work in Regulation 9; and persons treated as unavailable for work in Regulation 10 of SI 1987 No. 1967. Among those listed in Regulation 10 to be treated as unavailable for work are students (Regulation 10 (1) (h) (4)) and claimants who are for various reasons deemed 'voluntarily unemployed' (Regulation 10 (1) (a), (b), (c), (d), (e) and (f)).

57   S20 (1) (b). The claimants income must be below his 'applicable amount' which is discussed below.

58   S22 (6).

59   Capital of under £3,000 is disregarded, but between £3,000 and £8,000 income of £1 per week for every £250 is assumed (Regulations 45 and 53 of SI 1987 No. 1967). Some capital is ignored, including the claimant's home.

60   S22 of the 1986 Act and Regulation 17 of SI 1987 No. 1967. Rates of personal allowances, premiums and housing costs are detailed in schedule 2 to the Regulations, which is periodically amended by Secretary of State to uprate benefits.

61 S21 (1) of the 1986 Act.

62 SI 1987 No. 1967 Sch. 1 (Part I).

63 S20 (3) (a) of the 1986 Act, as amended by the Social Security Act 1988 S4.

64 S20 (4A) of the 1986 Act added by the Social Security Act 1988 S4.

65 Regulation 13A (3) (a) of SI 1987 No. 1967, and Schedule 1A Part I.

66 Regulation 13A (3) (b) of SI 1987 No. 1967, and Schedule 1A Part II. The Child Benefit
    Extension period is discussed below.

67 S20 (4B) of the 1986 Act.

68 S20 (4C) of the 1986 Act.

69 SI 1987 No. 1967 Sch. 1 (Part I).

70 S25 (3) of the Education Reform Act 1988.

71 SA3 Department of Employment Guide 13 – YTS Bridging Allowance.

72 S2 (1) (aa) of the Child Benefit Act 1975 as amended, and Regulation 7D(1) of the Child
    Benefit (General) Regulations 1976 as amended (SI 1976/965).

73 Regulation 7D(2) Child Benefit (General) Reg. 1976 as amended.

74 S20 (7) – (8H) of the Social Security Act 1986 outlines the basic entitlement conditions to
    HB. Most full-time students have been excluded from HB since September 1990 (Reg. 48
    (A) (1) Housing Benefit Regulations SI 1987/971).

75 Regulation 10 of SI 1987/1971 defines payments which are eligible rent for HB purposes,
    and those which are not.

76 Regulation 11 (2) of SI 1987/1971 as amended. The local authority must consider the
    merits of individual cases and can only operate the 'rent stop' if the accommodation is too
    large or expensive and it is *appropriate* to restrict, your eligible rent. A blanket 'rent stop'
    policy can be challenged by judicial review in the Court of Session.

77 Reg. 11 (4), (5) of SI 1987/1971.

78 Regulation 63 of SI 1987/1971.

79 Definition of non-dependants is a negative one, in that it includes all those who do not fit
    into other categories in Regulation 3 (2) of SI 1987/1971.

80 During the course of our study the 5 new bands came into force on 1st April 1992.

81 S21 (4) Social Security Act 1986.

82 S21 (5) Social Security Act 1986.

83 The Social Security Act 1986 Part III sets out the framework for the Social Fund, but much
    of the detail is in *directions* or *guidance* by the Secretary of State and published in the Social
    Fund Manual. The directions, but not the guidance, in the Social Fund Manual are binding
    on Social Fund Officers.

84 Direction 5 of SF Manual.

85 In exercising their discretion as to whether to make a payment under the discretionary
    Social Fund the SFO must have regard to all the circumstances of the case, and in
    particular: the nature, extent and urgency of the need; the existence of resources from
    which the need may be met; the possibility that some other person or body may meet the
    need; where the payment is repayable (Budget and Crisis Loans) the likelihood of
    repayment; and the relevant budget allocation. (S33 (9) of the 1986 Act as amended).

86 The allocation is made under S32 (8A) of the 1986 Act.

87 Direction 42 of SF Manual.

88 Direction 40 of SF Manual.

89   Paragraph 2015 of SF Manual.

90   Direction 25 of SF Manual and Direction 4 of SF Manual. You must also establish that you would have less than £500 capital if you bought the item applied for (Direction 27).

91   Paragraph 6013 SF Manual.

92   Direction 29 of SF Manual.

93   SF Direction 8. You must also establish that you would be left with less than £500 capital if you were to buy what the loan is for. (SF Direction 9).

94   Direction 2 of SF Manual.

95   See Note 85 above.

96   Direction 12 of SF Manual.

97   Direction 14 of SF Manual.

98   Direction 3 (a) SF Manual.

99   Direction 3 (b) of SF Manual.

100   Direction 23 of SF Manual.

101   Abolition of Domestic Rates (Scotland) Act 1987.

102   Regulation 46 (1) of Community Charge Benefit (General) Regulations SI 1989/1321.

103   S21 (5A) and 20 (8E) (a) (b) of Social Security Act 1986 as amended.

104   S21 (5B) and 20 (8E) (c) of Social Security Act 1986 as amended.

Social work responsibilities to young people

105   Code of Guidance 2.9.

106   Code of Guidance 2.10.

107   Code of Guidance 2.11.

108   S12 (2) (a) of Social Work (Scotland) Act 1968.

109   Ibid S12 (2) (b).

110   Ibid S94 (1).

111   Review of Child Care Law in Scotland, published by H.M.S.O., October 1990.

112   Ibid Recommendation (2).

113   S16 – 18, 20, 24 – 26, and 28 and 29 of the 1968 Act.

114   S10 and S12.

115   S26.

116   S11.

117   S20 of the 1968 Act.

118   Ibid S20A.

119   Child Care Law Review Recommendation 24.

120   Ibid Recommendation 25.

121   Ibid Recommendation 23.

122   S24 of Children's Act 1989.

123   S5A (4) of the 1968 Act, added by S52 of the 1990 Act.

124   S5A of the 1968 Act as amended.

125   S12A of the 1968 Act, added by S55 of the 1990 Act.

126   "Caring for People: Community Care in the Next Decade and Beyond", published for the Secretary of State for Health, Social Security, Scotland and Wales; London: H.M.S.O. November 1989, Chapter I: 'Better Community Care Services'.

2. The Teams Included In The Study With Examples Of Good Practice

Social Work Area Team 'A': Lothian Region

This social work area team is centrally located in a large city. Due to its setting it encounters many homeless people of all ages and needs. It has a large staff, and liaises successfully with many statutory and voluntary organisations including the housing department, the police, the DSS, and a large number of voluntary organisations which provide services to homeless people.

The team works with homeless people, and has built up a wealth of experience and contacts in this field. For those young people who are allocated as cases, social workers (despite restrictive case loads) offer significant amounts of support. Where feasible, an attempt is made to enable other agencies to manage young people in supported accommodation.

In general, the pattern of case management is similar to that in other social work teams. Only extremely vulnerable young people reach case status, and a combination of limited resources and the young person's immaturity prohibit effective management. The bulk of young people are assisted on a duty basis, contact is sporadic, and workers usually have to react to crisis presentations.

Operating a 'Bail Scheme' workers attempt to find accommodation places for offenders facing court appearances and thus prevent potential imprisonment (likely if a person is NFA), whilst probation workers attempt to organise accommodation (only one component of intervention) for the person's release from prison.

Social Work Area Team 'B': Lothian Region

This social work area team is located within an urban area of Lothian Region.

The team recognise that youth homelessness is now a significant problem in the area, and is a major presenting factor on intake. The team encounter a number of local referrals, a result of family breakdowns or young people who have previously been in care. However, its proximity to a major city centre, and the considerable number of bed and breakfast establishments in the area, means that the majority of young homeless people are drawn from outwith the area.

All young homeless people who self-refer are seen by a social worker on an intake duty system. In order to maximise their advice and information role, the team has an advice desk with up-to-date information available in the interview room. Where the need for accommodation appears to be a primary factor, referrals are made to the homeless person's officer at the housing department, with the young person often being escorted.

Good liaison arrangements exist with several voluntary agencies which provide good quality accommodation or specialist skills suitable for young people. The social work and housing boundaries are not congruent, and at the area team level links are seen to be poor and undeveloped.

Social Work Area Team 'C': Strathclyde Region

This social work area team is located within an urban area of Strathclyde Region. The team members recognise that they are able to help only a few young people, and they are rarely able to engage in case work. Where positive intervention does take place, social workers make considerable efforts to re-integrate the young person into the family home, or alternatively, work with families who are experiencing difficulties in order to prevent the young person leaving home. This work is undertaken on the intake system and with the consent of the young person.

Good practice is impeded in this area team for two main reasons. First, social workers are forced to work in a housing environment in which "no services are available to young people who are homeless". Second, the team has a high turnover of social workers, who "join the team directly from college prior to moving to another area". Many social workers have limited experience and little knowledge of the local area.

Moreover, social workers often resort to giving young people monies under Section 12 of the Social Work Scotland Act 1968 in order that they can travel out of the area in search of accommodation, and buy some food. In many instances, this represents the extent of social work intervention.

Social Work Area Team 'D': Strathclyde Region

The unique aspect of this social work area team is that it contributes to a joint project with the district council housing department. The social work side of the project includes a senior social worker and homemakers. Workers offer support to vulnerable young people in specialist district council tenancies. The majority of cases include child care issues, which prevent a wider remit being adopted (see also Team 'H').

Specialist Social Work Team 'E': Strathclyde Region

This specialist social work team receives core funding from Strathclyde Region Social Work Department. The team provide a social work support service to young people in temporary accommodation. This group include many young people who have been or are in danger of becoming homeless.

The team work principally with 16 and 17 year old males and females. Between December 1989 and December 1990 it had contact with 570 young people. Of those who received help, 30% moved on to an independent tenancy, 20% made a planned and supported return to their family home, and 50% "disappeared". It is recognised that a considerable proportion of those who "disappeared" return through the system at a later date.

The team receive referrals from the housing department and area team social workers.

There are several examples of good practice undertaken by this team.

(1) Intervention is focused on the young person's own needs and development pace. In other words, workers do not offer 'standardised' services.

(2) Responsibilities for case management are shared between a qualified social worker and a designated support worker. The social worker manages the case, advocates on behalf of the young person and focuses on any behavioural difficulties of the young person. The support worker has more regular contact with the young person and predominantly works on a range of practical issues.

(3) Young people do not regard this team as an area social work team, and workers are not seen as social workers. Young people strike up good working relationships with team members under these conditions.

Good practice is impeded by two factors. First, the team receives many inappropriate referrals by both the housing department and the social work department and time is wasted in attempting to make appropriate re-referrals. Young people often give up under these circumstances and are consequently 'lost to the system'. Second, the setting is not helpful because the offices are located in an 'unsafe' area which young people are reluctant to visit at night.

Specialist Voluntary Organisation 'F': Lothian Region

This voluntary organisation, now part-funded by Lothian Region Social Work Department, offers a range of services which are of value to particularly vulnerable groups amongst the young homeless or potentially homeless population.

(1) Three residential units offering supported accommodation for a maximum of eight young people, with a 24 hour on-call emergency service for these units.

(2) A care package based on a case work model, including an intensive counselling service where appropriate.

(3) An informal drop-in project for young people.

(4) Group work designed to help young people develop social skills.

(5) An after-care service for people who have left care, or other residential units, and are now in the wider community.

This agency aims to help people progress to a situation whereby they can manage 'inter-dependently' within the community. The predominant client group is drawn from those young people who have experienced behavioural difficulties in the care system. At the time of study approximately 30 young people were using the services offered by this agency.

Since the project began, the demand for the supported accommodation has always outstripped the number of places available. Between April 1990 and September 1991, 85 referrals were made for supported accommodation, the majority of which were 16 or 17 years old. 32% of all referrals were made from social work area teams, and 22% from the Stopover project in Edinburgh. The remainder were referred from a range of both voluntary and statutory agencies.

Examples of good practice include:–

(1) Field social workers act in tandem with residential support workers. This enables a division of responsibilities according to the skills each has to offer. The support worker makes regular reports to the field worker.

(2) No time limit is set upon the resolution of cases. The agency recognises that individuals develop at different speeds and require a range of flexible support and counselling. The agency aims to work with the client towards the goal of being able to manage "inter-dependently within the wider community". Support is provided to facilitate this ultimate move.

(3) Whilst the agency does require clients to leave the supported accommodation when mistakes are made, relationships with the young person are maintained. Here workers aim either to help the young person move to alternative accommodation, or help re-integrate the client to the supported accommodation on a new contract.

(4) Where the field social worker holds responsibility for the client (as opposed to an area team social worker), strenuous efforts are made to coordinate all joint work.

However, two practice dilemmas can also be identified. Since the agency is one of the few which offers supported accommodation to young people in Lothian Region, too much time is spent dealing with referrals which are either inappropriate for the service available, or cannot be met as few vacancies exist. There is a clear need for a more effective screening process to be developed, and better liaisons to be established with referring agencies to ensure that staff time is not wasted.

The second dilemma faced by this agency concerns decisions to terminate or transfer a case held. Workers tend to carry cases for significant periods to ensure that the young person is managing in the wider community. Better links need to be established with other voluntary agencies which can help people in the community.

Specialist Social Work Team 'G': Strathclyde Region

This specialist social work team, funded by Strathclyde Region Social Work Department, offers an "open door out-of-hours service to teenagers and their families, which may at times include the use of a small number of beds".

The project works with teenagers and their families who are experiencing relationship difficulties at home. The project stresses the "normality of facing difficulties with such complicated relationships", and strives to facilitate their resolution, and hence prevent the teenager becoming homeless. This includes the provision of respite accommodation and counselling. With those young people who cannot resolve their familial disputes, work is undertaken to help the young person progress towards a position in which they can manage independently.

Referrals are made by teenagers themselves, by their families, the social work department, the housing department, the police, and the Citizens' Advice Bureau. In 1989, the project responded to 296 referrals (157 individuals) of male and female teenagers aged between 14 and 18, the majority being 14 to 16 years old. Of this number 137 individuals were able to remain in the family home or with relatives, or made a successful move into a hostel or their own accommodation.

One of the many unique services this agency provides, is a "follow-up service" is provided. Relationships are maintained with families for up to 2 years after initial contact, with advice and counselling available, in an attempt to ensure that further familial crises do not arise.

This agency offers a unique service aimed at negotiating solutions to relationship difficulties experienced by young people and their parents. For those young people who cannot return home, a range of services are made available to help them progress towards a position of independence.

Some of the cases held by this agency are managed independently; in other instances, project workers collaborate with statutory and voluntary agencies and agree to offer services where appropriate. The project's relationships with both the housing and social work departments are good.

Housing Department Specialist Team 'H': Strathclyde Region

This specialist team consists of 4 support workers who have access to 30 flats for temporary accommodation and 34 furnished and scatter flats. About half of this stock is available for young homeless people. The support workers assist young people to move into the flats, assess their needs and offer advice on budgeting, self-care and, in some instances, personal problems. While most difficult cases are normally referred to the social work area team 'D' the support workers are reluctant to let cases go and their work with some clients is indistinguishable from that which would be provided by a social worker. There is good collaboration between teams 'H' and 'D' and managers have regular meetings and case conferences for the most difficult cases.

Specialist Social Work Team 'I': Lothian Region

This specialist social work team, funded by Lothian Region Social Work Department, helps young homeless people or potentially homeless people gain access to and maintain a range of accommodation types.

Receiving referrals from a broad spectrum of agencies, three workers attempt to match the young person's presenting needs with *appropriate* lodgings in the private rented sector. Accommodation is usually paid for through a combination of housing benefit and a lodger's contribution from their income support entitlements.

Recognising that background reports on young people are often sketchy, workers complete a comprehensive assessment and negotiate which areas of concern (e.g. finances, expectations, rules and responsibilities) will be focused on through intervention. The team has strong links with those agencies that provide and monitor lodgings accommodation.

In 1990, between 230 and 240 young people were referred to this team, of whom about 60 young people were placed and supported in lodgings. Benefit restrictions have virtually excluded all under 18 year olds from using the service. The vast bulk of referrals come from the 'care system', for young people who have not been able to manage independently or have attempted to return unsuccessfully to the family home.

This team is able to facilitate many successful placements on behalf of the young person for a number of reasons. First, the young people do not consider the teams' workers to be social workers. Second, team members have specialised training and a wealth of experience in helping young people. They are committed to working with young people even when they are at their most difficult. Third, the workers have small case-loads and can invest a considerable amount of time on individual cases. Fourth, good liaison arrangements are held with a variety of agencies. Finally, the team use a 'pot-pourri' of accommodation resources (including private lodgings and their own stock). This flexibility enables them to match a young person's needs to a specific service. Once a young person has been placed in a residential unit, support is provided where needed for up to two years.

3. Selected Bibliography

1. General

Bramley, G. (1988) The definition and measurement of homelessness. In Bramley, G. *et al.* Homelessness and the London Housing Market. School of Advanced Urban Studies, Bristol.

Drake, M. O'Brien, M. and Biebuyck, T. (1981) Single and Homeless. H.M.S.O., London.

Drake, M. (1989) Fifteen years of homelessness in the UK. Housing Studies, Vol. 4, No. 2, pp. 119-127.

Glasgow Council for the Single Homeless (1990) Single Homelessness and Housing Need in Glasgow: a report on GCSH's survey of hostel residents. Glasgow.

Greve, J. and Currie, E. (1990) Homelessness in Britain. Joseph Rowntree Foundation.

Greve, J. (1991) Homelessness in Britain. Joseph Rowntree Foundation.

Johnson, B. *et al* (1991) A Typology of Homelessness. A report to Scottish Homes: Edinburgh.

Joint Charities Group on Homelessness (1989) Who Says There's No Housing Problem? Facts and Figures on Housing and Homelessness. Shelter.

Thomas, A. and Niner, P. (1989) Living in temporary accommodation: a survey of homeless people. H.M.S.O.: London.

2. Social Work

Audit Commission (1986) Making a Reality of Community Care. H.M.S.O.: London.

Barclay, P. M. (Chairman) (1982) Social workers: their role and tasks (when young people leave care). Bedford Square Pegs: London.

D.o.E. (1989) Caring for People: Community care in the next decade and beyond. H.M.S.O.: London.

Griffiths, R. (1988) Community care: agenda for action. A report to the Secretary of State for Social Services. H.M.S.O.: London.

Morris Committee (1975) Housing and Social Work a Joint Approach. The report of the Morris Committee on links between housing and social work. H.M.S.O.: Edinburgh.

Stewart, G. and Stewart, J. (1982) Social Work and Homelessness Social Work and Homelessness Group, University of Lancaster.

3. The Law

Bonner *et al.* (1991) Non-Means Tested Benefits: The Legislation. Child Poverty Action Group. Sweet and Maxwell: London.

Dilnot, A. and Webb, S. (1988) The 1988 social security reforms. Fiscal Studies. August. pp 26-53.

Mesher, J. (1991) Income Related Benefits: The Legislation. Child Poverty Action Group. Sweet and Maxwell: London.

Mullen, T. (1987) A Guide to Judicial Review in Scotland. Shelter (Scotland): Edinburgh.

Scottish Office (1990) Review of Child Care Law in Scotland. H.M.S.O.: Edinburgh.

Scottish Office Environment Department (1991) Homelessness: Part II of the Housing (Scotland) Act 1987 Code of Guidance – Scotland. Scottish Office: Edinburgh.

Ward, M. and Zebedee, J. (1991) Guide to Housing Benefit and Community Charge Benefit 1991/92. SHAC and Institute of Housing: London.

Watchman, P. and Robson, P. (1989) Homelessness and The Law. Planning Exchange: Glasgow.

Watchman, P. (1991) The Housing (Scotland) Act 1987. W. Green & Son: Edinburgh.

4. Homelessness and the Local Authority

Audit Commission (1989) Housing the Homeless: The Local Authority Role. H.M.S.O.: London.

Caskie, K. (1990) Some Chance: Local Authority Response to Homelessness and Housing Need Among Young People. Shelter (Scotland): Edinburgh.

Duguid, G. (1990) Homelessness in Scotland – A Study of Policy and Practice. Scottish Office, Central Research Unit Paper. Scottish Office: Edinburgh.

Niner, P. (1989) Homelessness in Nine Local Authorities. H.M.S.O.: London.

Thornton, R. (1990) The New Homeless: The Crisis of Youth Homelessness and Response of the Local Housing Authorities. SHAC: London.

5. Young People

Abrahams, C. and Mungall, R. (1989) Housing Vulnerable Single Homeless People. National Children's Home: London.

Caskie, K. *et al.* (1991) Living on the Borderline: Homeless Young Scots in London. Shelter (Scotland): Edinburgh.

Chalmers, C. (ed.) (1990) Homeless Voices: The Experience of Homeless Teenagers in Scotland. Scottish Child: Edinburgh.

Doogan, K. (1988) Falling off the treadmill: the causes of youth homelessness. In Bramley, G. *et al.* Homelessness and the London Housing Market. School of Advanced Urban Studies, Bristol.

Furlong, A. and Cooney, G. H. (1992) Getting on their bikes: Teenagers leaving home in Scotland in the 1980s. Journal of Social Policy, 19, 4, pp. 535-551.

Jones, G. (1990) Household Formation Among Young Adults in Scotland. Scottish Homes Discussion Paper No. 2. Scottish Homes: Edinburgh.

Kileen, D. (1984) Homeless Young People in Glasgow, Shelter (Scotland).

Kirk, D. *et al.* (1991) Excluding Youth: Poverty Among Young People Living Away From Home. Bridges Project and Edinburgh Centre for Social Welfare Research, University of Edinburgh.

Scottish Council for the Single Homeless (1989) Young People – Managing the Future. Scottish Council for the Single Homeless.

Stein, A. A. and Carey, K. (1986) Leaving Care. Basil Blackwell.

Strathclyde Poverty Alliance (1992) Youth Destitution in Strathclyde, S.P.A., 162 Buchanan Street, Glasgow G1 2LL.

Printed in Scotland for H.M.S.O. (18023)
DJ 287528 C15 1/93